THE KIDS' SUMMER FUN BOOK

First edition for the United States, its territories and dependencies, and
Canada published in 2011 by Barron's Educational Series, Inc.

Copyright © 2011 Elwin Street Productions
Conceived and produced by Elwin Street Productions
144 Liverpool Road
London N1 1 LA
United Kingdom
www.elwinstreet.com

All inquiries should be addressed to:
Barron's Educational Series, Inc.
250 Wireless Blvd.
Hauppauge, NY 11788
www.barronseduc.com

ISBN-13: 978-0-7641-4581-0
ISBN-10: 0-7641-4581-9

Library of Congress Control Number: 2010931490

The activities described in this book are to be carried out with parental
supervision at all times. Every effort has been made to ensure the safety of the
activities detailed. Neither the author nor the publishers shall be liable or
responsible for any harm or damage done allegedly arising from any
information or suggestion in this book.

Picture credits:
Alamy: pp. 104; Corbis: pp. 69, 71; Dreamstime: pp. 11 (bottom), 15 (right),
21 (right), 23 (right), 27, 28, 33 (right), 34, 42, 45 (top), 77, 98, 99, 108, 123;
Getty Images: pp. 8, 19, 78, 83; iStock images: pp. 11 (top), 15 (left), 21 (left),
51, 55, 56, 58, 93, 113, 116; Photos to go: pp. 61, 97.

Illustrations by: David Eaton

Printed in China

9 8 7 6 5 4 3 2 1

THE KIDS' SUMMER FUN BOOK

GREAT GAMES, ACTIVITIES, AND ADVENTURES FOR THE ENTIRE FAMILY

CLAIRE GILLMAN
& SAM MARTIN

BARRON'S

CONTENTS

INTRODUCTION 6

1 ON THE WATER

Stay cool and fresh with water-based activities for the whole family to enjoy

2 OUT OF DOORS

You'll have hours of fun in the sun with these great ways to spend active days outside

3 SPORTS AND GAMES

With loads of fun sports and games to suit everyone, it's time to get competitive

4 CRAFTS AND ACTIVITIES

Let your creativity run wild with these fantastic things to make and do

5 FEASTING

The hardest thing about these delicious recipes is choosing which to try first!

INDEX

INTRODUCTION

When the spring days brighten and the afternoons begin to grow long, you know that summer has finally arrived. The sunshine heralds the beginning of adventurous afternoons, days of discovery, and hours of creative fun. These days you and your friends might be tempted to spend your free time watching television or maybe playing a computer game, but think of all the fun you could be having in the great outdoors. Rediscover the classic fun and games the summer months can offer—after all, can a day spent in front of the television really compare with a day spent with your friends in a treehouse, especially one that you built yourself?

All it takes is a little imagination to create a summer wonderland full of fun and promise. Grassy fields are your sport arenas, sandy beaches are long-lost pirate hideouts, and your very own backyard becomes a fantasy world ripe for exploration. With a few friends, some easy-to-find equipment, and a thirst for fun, you can make sure you have a summer to remember.

You'll find plenty of great ideas to fill the long sunny days, with activities for adventuring and exploring as well as more creative things to do. After reading this book your head will be close to bursting with ideas as you try to decide whether to hike to the top of the nearest hills and test your wilderness skills, search the beach for long-lost treasure or keepsakes, or build your own kite to fly in the park.

Wherever you are and whatever you enjoy doing, there is always plenty to keep you entertained. If you're feeling energetic, why not waterski or head into the woods and see if you can find your way around without a compass. Or if you're feeling inquisitive, go and explore: the rock pools and woodland canopies are miniature worlds waiting to be discovered. For the competitive there are plenty of games to play, from softball to tug-of-war, and when you find yourself in need of food and refreshment after a long day of adventuring, *The Kids' Summer Fun Book* offers loads of delicious recipes that are easy to make and perfect for sharing with your friends and family.

Whether on vacation or at home, there is always plenty to do: *The Kids' Summer Fun Book* is every child's guide to fun all the way through the summer months.

HOW TO USE THIS BOOK

Some of the summer activities in this book are more tricky or time-consuming than others, and you may want to make sure you have a group of family or friends gathered to give you a helping hand. Every activity is graded for difficulty and shows the amount of time that you will need to be able to complete the activity. So, whether you have just a few minutes to fill in your backyard or a whole day to spend by the water, you'll never be stuck without anything to do.

One sun symbol indicates a project or activity that is simple to do, whether on your own or with friends; two symbols indicate where you might need a bit of skill to accomplish it; and three symbols may require a fair bit of practice to get right, or perhaps a few pairs of helping hands to complete.

ON THE WATER

When the weather gets hot, the water becomes
very enticing. Whether you're heading to the beach,
lake, or river, there are so many activities to keep the
whole family entertained that you'll need more than
one day to do them all. The following pages are just
a few of the best ideas. From the sand and surf of
the beach to the trees and hidey-holes of the creek
or the thrill of watersports on the lake, spending
time on and by the water opens up a world
full of excitement and adventure.

BUILD A SAND CASTLE

Nothing defines a day at the beach like building a sand castle. In fact, it could be the ultimate summer activity—that one thing you look forward to every year and the one thing you lament as the tides come in and the vacation comes to a close. Building with sand is fun, relaxing, creative, and attention grabbing. It's also something you can do on your own, or you can get the whole family to pitch in and help.

| SKILL LEVEL | ◉ |
| TIME NEEDED | 1 hour |

You can use the simplest tools like a plastic pail and a shovel, or you can get serious and bring in a raft of clay sculpting tools like trowels, pointed sticks, chisels, and brushes. You might like to bring plastic pails and containers of varying sizes—large trash can-sized ones for the base and varying smaller containers to build up (individual yogurt containers make for good tops). And you can collect shells to decorate the rims of towers and walls.

YOU WILL NEED

A variety of different-sized containers

A small shovel

CHOOSING YOUR SITE

The right type of sand is the key to any sand castle. It has to be wet but not so wet that it falls apart. Here's a good test: Find the high-tide line where the darker, wet sand begins to blend into the dry sand that blows easily. Then pick up a fistful of wet sand, compress it into a ball and roll it along the beach. If it remains intact, it's good for building. If it falls apart, it's not wet enough.

Next, find a good flat location where you can build—a good spot is usually a bit further up the beach from the wet sand you need to build with. Not only will the land be flatter farther from the tide but you'll be safe from rogue waves or high tide. If you decide to build on a spot well beyond the tide line, you'll need to carry a supply of wet sand up to your building site, so get the shovels and pails, and start digging and hauling! Just pile the wet sand up when you get to your site. Or fill up a pail with water and mix it with the dry sand for more building materials.

Before you start building, pour several pails of water on the area where you plan to erect your castle. Then pack down the area and smooth it to make a firm, flat platform foundation.

TOP TIPS

Carve sand in a gentle shaving method rather than trying to remove large chunks.

Wear sunscreen and a hat! Big sand castles can take hours to build and hours under the hot sun can give you a bad sunburn.

Keep a spray bottle filled with water handy, so that you can keep the surface sand wet. This helps prevent the sand from crumbling during the building process.

All sand castles start with a central structure or tower. Then you can build out from that by connecting walls to outer turrets and a circular wall. Use the following steps to get started.

1 Fill your largest container with sand and compress it down as much as possible to remove any air spaces or pockets of dry sand.

2 Turn the container upside down on the center of your foundation and tap the sides and top with your hands to loosen the sand from the insides of the container. Lift the container up and off the molded sand structure. This is your first storey. Don't worry if some sand falls away. This can be fixed later.

3 Continue packing sand in smaller containers and stacking them up to make the central tower as tall as you like.

4 Once you get it to the height you want, get out the detail tools (plastic knives, spoons, and forks work just as well as anything) and start carving in windows, turrets, stairs, arrow slits, ramps, and whatever else your imagination comes up with. Start at the top and work your way down so falling sand doesn't destroy things you've already created.

5 After the central tower is built, mold walls with your hands. They should be wide at the bottom and thinner as they go up. Carve arched doorways into walls. Outer towers can be built in the same way the central tower was.

6 Once you're happy with the structure, decorate it with seaweed, shells, beach glass, and other found objects.

BEACH-COMBING

Hunting along the surf and dunes of a beach for flotsam and jetsom—the lost, discarded treasures that wash up on shore—can provide hours of adventure as well as a few tokens you can take back home or hang around your neck for good luck.

SKILL LEVEL	●
TIME NEEDED	½–1 hour

YOU WILL NEED

A local tide chart

A bag

A small rake or shovel

1 Check local tide charts. The best time to go is during low tide.

2 To increase your chances of finding good stuff, check peninsular sandbars (which will be visible when the tide is out).

3 Try and find an area of the beach that isn't too crowded. The days after big storms are also good times to hunt.

4 Use a small rake or shovel to dig out possible shells and other treasures when you see the tips of them sticking up.

CRAB FISHING

Casting out a good old line and a hook is one way to catch critters at the beach, but it's not the only way. Setting crab traps—also known as crab pots—are far more relaxing. Throw some bait in, lower the trap, then go build a sand castle. Come back later and you'll have an interesting clawed friend to study for a while.

SKILL LEVEL	●
TIME NEEDED	2–3 hours

EQUIPMENT First you have to find a crab pot. If this is a one-time fishing experiment, get mom or dad and go ask a local bait retailer if you can rent one or two for the day. They're essentially large wire crates with holes and trapdoors for the crabs to get into but not get out. You might need a fishing license so check into that first.

FINDING A SPOT The best time to fish for crabs is early in the morning. The best place is off a pier where the water is a bit deeper (but not too deep) rather than off shore. Once you have your wire trap, bait or "set" it with mussels or chicken necks placed at the center of the pot and secured with a wire or cord. Then lower the pot into the water over the side of the pier until it sits on the ocean floor. Tie the trap to the pier and wait. You should have a specimen by lunch time at the latest. Don't forget to let your crab go before you leave.

DIG FOR TREASURE

Pirates and the beach go together like seagulls and tuna fish sandwiches so why not create your own Treasure Island complete with buried treasure. Unless you're fortunate enough to run across a real map in a nearby sea cave, you'll have to create your own "X Marks the Spot" and the treasure under it. Or get mom or dad to set you up.

SKILL LEVEL	●
TIME NEEDED	1 hour

1 Gather some rocks that are nugget-shaped, and paint them gold and silver. This is the actual treasure. Put them in a shoe box. This is the treasure chest.

2 Find a location far from the crowds and, using your shovel, dig a hole about three feet deep to bury the "treasure chest." After you've filled the hole, mark the spot with an X made of stones, palm fronds, or sticks. (To add a challenge to the game, get a parent to bury the treasure so you have to find it first.)

3 Now make your treasure map. After you've marked the spot of the treasure, mark it down on a piece of paper and draw the basic landmark shapes around it—a tree, a lifeguard stand, the ocean.

4 Then count your steps to the nearest landmark and write down how many steps it took to get there. At the same time, draw a dotted line from the tree to the "X."

5 Make your way back to your spot on the beach, counting steps and drawing dotted lines as you go until you have an accurate locator to the treasure.

6 Find the treasure and dig it up!

YOU WILL NEED

Rocks

Gold and silver paint

A shoe box

A shovel

Pen and paper

TOP TIP

Once you have the master map done, you can create alternative maps by leaving clues to the location for prospective treasure hunters instead of giving them the map outright.

MESSAGE IN A BOTTLE

Think of a message in a bottle and it might conjure up visions of desperate castaways trying to get off their deserted islands. But they can be a fun way to pass messages among your friends along rivers and small bodies of water. Or cast it into the sea and a stranger in a far-off land just might get your message!

SKILL LEVEL	●
TIME NEEDED	½ hour

1 Write a note. Always write in pencil because it won't fade or smudge in the elements. Be sure to put your name, date, and address so whoever finds it can send you a note through the mail. Write something about your hometown or your hopes and dreams.

2 Staple or glue a ribbon to a corner of the note. Then roll up your note around the pencil.

3 Holding the other end of the ribbon, drop your note and pencil into the bottle.

4 Secure the ribbon to the bottom of your cork (again with glue or the stapler), and press the cork firmly into the bottle until it's snug.

5 Heat the wax in a pot. Once it has melted, dip the corked end of your bottle in to seal it.

6 Then toss the bottle into the water.

YOU WILL NEED

A thick glass bottle with a cork

Wax

Paper

Ribbon

A stapler or glue

A pencil

A pot

DID YOU KNOW?

During the 1500s in England sending a message in a bottle was a royally sanctioned means of communication. In fact, floating messages were used by the British fleet to Queen Elizabeth I and she employed an official "Uncorker of Ocean Bottles." It was a crime for anyone else to open a bottle with a message in it. Later, in the United States, Benjamin Franklin charted ocean currents by dropping bottles into the Gulf Stream and finding out where they went when the bottles were discovered and returned to him from afar through the mail.

TOP TIP

Make sure you throw the bottle into the water when the tide is going out so the bottle will go out to sea instead of ending up a few yards down the shore.

MAKING A SAND BOTTLE

Here's another fun beach art project involving perhaps the most available material at the beach other than water—sand. It's a great way to create a beautiful souvenir to remind you of a fun day out at the beach. Plus, it's a good way to recycle soda bottles, empty jars, and any other glass containers you might find floating or laying around. Just make sure any bottles you find don't contain any messages.

SKILL LEVEL ●

TIME NEEDED 1 hour

1 Cover your piece of wood with the paper and cover the paper with sand. Remove any pebbles or other detritus from the sand.

2 Roll a piece of colored chalk across the sand until the sand has completely changed to that color. This should take about five minutes depending on how much sand you have. Don't worry if some of the sand falls off, but try to keep most of it on your work surface.

3 When the sand is the color you want it, pour it into the bottle using the paper it's on as a funnel.

4 Repeat these steps until you have several colors of sand layered in your bottle and the sand is filled all the way to the top.

5 Put the bottle cap on the bottle as tightly as possible.

YOU WILL NEED

A large, flat piece of wood

Paper (newspaper works fine)

Sand

Various colors of chalk

Clear glass bottles or jars

A bottle cap

TOP TIP

If you don't have a bottle cap, leave a ½ inch gap between the sand and the top rim of the bottle and fill it with white glue. When it dries it will act like a stopper.

BEACH ART

Now that you've combed and dug and uncovered the treasures of things that wash up on the beach (see Beach-Combing, page 12), what can you do with them? Make stuff, of course. With all the shells, driftwood, and even sand you find after a morning of combing the shore, transform it into beach art for your room or a gift for mom or dad.

SKILL LEVEL	◉
TIME NEEDED	1½–2 hours

DRIFTWOOD SHIP SCULPTURE

Use pieces of driftwood to make a ship. This can be as big or as small as you want, but if it gets too big, you might need screws, nails, or other fasteners. Best to go small.

1 Remove any sand from the driftwood.

2 Paint an ocean scene—waves, seagulls, sun, clouds—on the flat piece of wood.

3 Glue a hull-shaped piece of wood to the front of the flat piece of wood.

4 Next glue on a smoke stack, maidenhead, poop deck, and any other extras you can imagine.

5 Paint portholes, an anchor, and other colors on the ship and give her a name.

6 Let it dry for at least an hour before taking it home.

YOU WILL NEED

Driftwood

1 flat, rectangular piece of wood

Wood glue

Paints

SCALLOPED SEASHELL

1 Rinse the salt and sand off of the shells in fresh water and set them out to dry.

2 Paint pictures of seagulls, waves, your dog, and anything else you can think of on the inside of each shell. Acrylics work best when you let one color dry before adding another.

3 When your art is finished— you'll know when—leave them to dry.

YOU WILL NEED

Seashells (chalkier, white shells work best)

Paints (acrylic works best)

Fresh water

Small paintbrush

EXPLORING SEA CAVES

If you find a beach surrounded by rocky limestone or chalky cliffs or rock piles, there's a good chance you can find a sea cave. And if you can find a sea cave, you're in for an adventure.

SKILL LEVEL	
TIME NEEDED	1½–2 hours

Sea caves are formed by the constant push and pull of the ocean waves. The rock has literally been eroded by the water over hundreds and thousands of years. Limestone and chalk are softer than most rocks so the likelihood of sea caves will be greater in places with this kind of geography, but the eroding power of water knows no boundaries. Sea caves can be found anywhere and they take on all kinds of shapes both above and below the waterline.

GETTING IN Exploring sea caves can be done in several different ways from snorkelling or kayaking into them during high tide to hiking through them at low tide. Sometimes you can discover caves that are only accessible underwater. You swim down and come up into a magical air filled cavern lit by blow holes on the ceiling of the cave. You have to know where these are by talking to the locals.

EXPLORING However you gain access to a cave, what you'll find inside verges on the otherworldly. Often there's white calcite glowing on the walls or sand deposits left by the high tide. Algae can line other parts of the cave. Stalagmites and stalactites form on ceilings and floors. And if it's rock pool discoveries you're after, you'll find life aplenty in a sea cave—and often it will be life you won't find in rock pools out in the bright sunlight, such as white barnacles and plant growth.

SAFETY Going into a cave requires a lot of care. Wet rocks can be slippery, and you have to pay special attention to the tides if you enter a cave at low tide. The force and power of waves coming into a cave becomes funneled and therefore amplified inside the small space. Wear waterproof shoes and consider taking a waterproof flashlight. If you swim in a cave, always pay close attention to tide swells. You don't want to swim down only to get pushed up against the rock by a swell. Timing is everything.

DID YOU KNOW?

One of the biggest sea caves in the world is found on Santa Cruz Island off the coast of California. It's called Painted Cave and is 1,318 feet (402 meters) long. The entrance to the cave is about 130 feet (40 meters) high.

FISHING

Because it's loaded with protein and vitamins, fish is an ideal food when out on a big adventure. But even if you don't plan to eat what you catch, fishing is a fun activity for a lazy summer's afternoon by the water. You can land one just to observe the underwater creature and then return it to its watery life.

SKILL LEVEL	◉
TIME NEEDED	1 hour

HOW TO MAKE A FISHING ROD

It's not the only way to catch a fish, but a fishing rod is the easiest. With a few supplies and a long straight stick, you can make a good one in less than an hour.

1 First, you need to find the right kind of stick. Bamboo works well because it can bend just enough without breaking if you catch a big one. Otherwise, a trimmed tree branch will do fine.

2 Cut a piece of line about the same length as your pole. Fishing line is strong and light, but very thin so fish can't see it in the water.

3 Tie the fishing line around the narrow end of your stick (the thicker end will be your handle).

4 Tie the line around your float about 1 foot (30 cm) from the end of the stick. Tie the hook to the very end of your line, and you're ready for some bait.

YOU WILL NEED

A 10-ft (3-m) long stick or bamboo cane

A fishing line

A fishing hook and float (old corks make good floats)

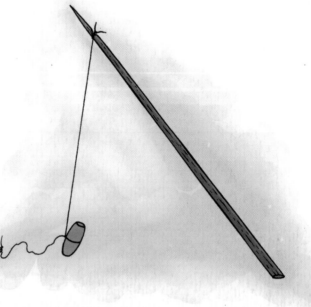

HOW TO BAIT A HOOK

You don't have to use professional hooks to catch a fish. Bent nails, pins, pieces of wire, and even sharp thorns work just as well.

1 To hook a worm, thread the hook through the head and run the hook through the body until the end is in the worm's tail.

2 If your worms aren't big enough to thread over the hook in this manner, you can use several worms—just be sure to fully cover the hook.

3 For insects, use a segment of thin metal wire and use it to wrap the bait around the hook. Do not damage the insect's body.

4 To bait small live fish or minnows, slide the hook in through the lower and upper lip or along the back (but avoid the spine). Both these techniques allow the fish to stay alive and swim as it normally would, which is appealing for the larger fish you're trying to catch.

SKILL LEVEL	
TIME NEEDED	5 minutes

YOU WILL NEED

A hook (or equivalent)

A worm, insect, or other bait

CHOOSING BAIT

If you can find a worm, use that to bait your hook. Fish love worms. If you can't find one, there are lots of other things a fish will gladly bite. Pay attention to your surroundings. More often than not fish dine on the insects and vegetation that is locally available. Your chances of catching a fish will be better if you tempt them with something familiar.

Potential Bait:

• Worm

• Grasshopper

• Fly

• Berry

• Bit of bread

• Cheese

• Pasta

ANGLING

Knowing where and how to fish is the next step on this adventure. With a home-made rod and simple bait, you're going to be limited to just dropping your line in the water. Even so, you can take a strategic approach to landing some swimmers. Here are a few pointers:

1 Look for stumps, large rocks, and vegetation—these are good places to drop your line. Fish are hunters too, so they're going to be hiding in these nooks and crannies to surprise their prey.

2 When fishing in the morning, especially in cooler weather, fish near the water's surface by tying your float closer to the hook.

3 In hotter weather, or later in the day, fish in deeper waters and try and get your line down as far as possible by tying your float closer to the rod.

4 Move the bait slowly through the water, as though it's alive and swimming. Fish prefer live prey.

5 When you see your float dip below the surface, that means you've got a bite! Pull up on the rod so the hook catches, and little by little pull your prey to shore. Don't pull so hard that the line breaks, or all your hard work will be for nothing.

SKILL LEVEL	◉
TIME NEEDED	1 hour

YOU WILL NEED

A hook (or equivalent)

A worm, insect, or other bait

LURES

If you can't find a worm, the grasshoppers keep eluding capture, and you've eaten all the other potential bait, use a lure. Fish will often bite something that just looks like their normal food. Simply attach a lure to your hook right above its end, in the hope that the fish will swallow the whole thing.

Potential Lures

• Feather

• Bottle cap

• Button

• Tin foil

EXPLORING ROCK POOLS

If you're lucky enough to find rock pools along your beach, then prepare to enter a fascinating world! They're great places to find animals and plants that are completely different from anything you'll see on land. As you investigate the pools, you can imagine you're the first person on a strange and mysterious planet, full of weird and wonderful creatures.

SKILL LEVEL	●
TIME NEEDED	1 hour

YOU WILL NEED

A plastic pail

A shovel

A plastic container with a flat clear bottom

Sandals

First, get your equipment ready. Take a plastic pail, a shovel for lifting out shells and turning over rocks, and a plastic container with a flat, clear bottom. You should also wear sandals. Not only will this give you extra grip on the slippery surfaces, but it'll also stop any little critters from nipping at your feet! To get a great view of the life in the pools, submerge your clear-bottomed container in the water and simply look through the bottom. Look out for crabs of all sorts hiding under rocks, and tiny fish and shrimp darting around in the water. Carefully turn over rocks to see what is hiding underneath, and don't forget to investigate the strange and colorful plants.

ANEMONES

Sea anemones are some of the most colorful creatures you're likely to find in a rock pool. Like barnacles, they can close up when threatened, at which point they look like brown slimy nodules on the rocks. But when they open out, they reveal hundreds of colorful tentacles that wave in the water. They may look pretty, but the tentacles are equipped with poison barbs, which sting small fish and other animals so that they can be drawn into the central body and eaten.

CRABS

Crabs are ten-legged crustaceans easily recognizable by their pincers. They are found all over the world and vary from less than an inch across the shell to almost 15 inches (38 cm) for deep sea varieties! They eat algae and small sea creatures, like tiny shrimps and worms. You may also find hermit crabs, which make their homes in the discarded shells of sea snails and other animals.

SHRIMP

Shrimp are crustaceans, like crabs, but have long thin bodies instead of short, round ones. Their legs are also long and thin, and they swim by waving their legs and tails, rather than scuttling around like crabs. There are thousands of different species visible all over the world. Larger shrimp can be cooked and eaten, but the small ones are more fun to observe.

If you lift a rock, you should always put it back where you found it, so the creatures' homes aren't disturbed. You should never remove living creatures from their habitat—if you do want to show others what you've found, call them over and let them see for themselves. You can collect empty shells and colorful stones that you find. These can be great decorations for your sand castles and sculptures.

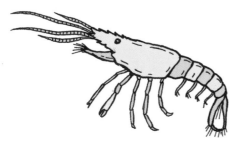

BARNACLES

Barnacles are small shellfish that grow on almost any underwater surface. When out of the water, they seal themselves up to look like small, white stars on the rocks. When they're covered by water again, their tops open out to reveal feathery fronds (actually the animal's legs) that capture plankton from the water for food. The legs will disappear quickly back into the shell if the water around them is disturbed, so you have to be very patient and careful if you want to see them feeding.

HOW TIDES WORK

The great thing about exploring rock pools is that they are constantly refreshed by the high tides. That means what you find one day will be gone and replaced with other wildlife the next. But why does the water level change in the ocean? It's all down to the moon—the gravitational force of the moon pulls the ocean toward it, creating a bulge of water when the moon is overhead. Interestingly, a bulge is created on the opposite side of the Earth too. Scientists believe this is because the Earth itself is pulled slightly toward the moon and away from the water on its opposite side! Because the moon makes a full rotation around the Earth every 24 hours and 50 minutes, there will be a high tide anywhere in the world every 12 hours and 25 minutes or so.

WARNING

There are always dangers when exploring so beware! Rock pools are submerged at high tide—it's the fresh water coming in with the tide that keeps them full of life. Be careful of wet slippery surfaces, and make sure you can easily get to dry land when the tide comes in!

SKIM STONES

Summer's day outings often end up by the water's edge, whether it's a pond, river, or lake. By throwing a flat stone into the water in a certain way, it's possible to make it bounce over the surface of the water. The key to skimming stones is the stone itself. The ideal skimming stone is a flat, oblong-shaped one with round edges. Perfectly round ones are good, but oblong ones give you a place to put your index finger to ensure you get the right spin.

SKILL LEVEL	
TIME NEEDED	5 minutes

1 Position the rock in your hand so that your thumb is on top of the rock, your index finger is wrapped around the front edge, and your middle and ring fingers are stabilizing it underneath.

2 Stand sideways to the water and pull your arm back, keeping the flat side of the rock parallel to the water.

3 Fling the rock with a side-arm motion. Bend your knees so you get low to the ground. You want the rock to hit the water at as low an angle as possible. Let the rock spin out of your hand and off the end of your index finger so that it spins horizontally, like a Frisbee landing on the water.

4 The harder your first throw is, the more the stone will "take off" after the first skip. This can be fun, but it can also limit any further skims. Practice to get the speed of throw just right so your stone skips several times.

YOU WILL NEED

Water

Flat, oblong-shaped rocks with round edges

DID YOU KNOW?

In Greek mythology, Hercules, the strongest man alive, was challenged to a discus-throwing competition by a young upstart. Hercules agreed, and hurled his discus so far out to sea that it landed on a nearby island. The boy, however, threw his discus like a skimming stone, so it bounced on the surface of the water and skipped out past the island. Hercules was so amused that legend says the two became close friends.

WARNING

Never skim stones in an area where there are swimmers. Skimmed stones can sometimes move erratically, and nobody likes a stone in the head.

MAKE AN ORIGAMI BOAT

Whether you're at a lake, pond, or river having a boat to float on the water is a great summer's activity. If you forgot to bring one along, it's easy to make your own out of paper.

SKILL LEVEL	◉
TIME NEEDED	10 minutes

The hobby of folding paper, more commonly known as origami, goes back many centuries. Although paper was introduced to Japan from China in the sixth century, folding paper to make models only became popular in the 1600s. The earliest designs were simple and started with boats and boxes, but now origami enthusiasts can make the most intricate and beautiful models of flowers, animals, and birds—and all without the use of a single pin, dot of glue, or a stapler!

YOU WILL NEED

A large, rectangular sheet of colored paper—the brighter the better!

1 Fold the paper in half widthways and make a crisp crease in the middle.

2 Bring each of the top corners in to meet in the middle, forming a triangular point. Crease the folds so that it lays flat.

3 Fold the bottom edge upward, so that the fold is level with the bottom of the triangle. Then flip it over and fold the other edge up in the same way.

4 Hold the triangle point-down, with your thumbs inside, and pull it open so that the sides come together. Press them flat and you should be left with a diamond shape.

5 At the open end of the diamond, fold each side down to make another triangle. Then pull it open as you did before to make another diamond.

6 Now all you have to do is turn the diamond upside-down and pull the sides away from the middle. With a little careful shaping, you'll end up with a beautiful paper boat with high prow and stern, and a triangular mast.

TOP TIP

To ensure you get a neat-looking model, make the folds as crisp as possible by running your fingernail along the edge to flatten the fold, and keep the corners neat by using the tip of your nail or a ballpoint pen to guide the fold to produce a sharp edge.

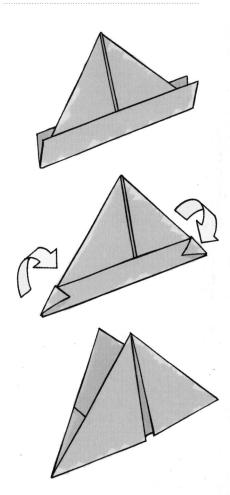

SWIMMING

Swimming is one of the best ways to keep in shape and get some energy out, as well as a refreshing way to relieve a hot summer's day. It's also helpful to know a few strokes in case your fishing boat springs a leak or you get caught in one of those pesky rip tides.

SKILL LEVEL	
TIME NEEDED	½–1 hour

There are two essential strokes every swimmer should know—the freestyle stroke or the crawl and the breast stroke. Get these down and you can move on to other, more challenging, swims like the butterfly stroke. With any stroke, swimmers should think about making themselves as streamlined as possible. Even the smallest resistance will tire you quickly so that means try not to splash much at all. Forward motion should be smooth, not jerky.

FREESTYLE OR CRAWL

This is the swim stroke everyone thinks about when they think of swimming: short back and forth "flutter" kick and windmill arm motion. The tricky part of this one is breathing, which you do by turning your head to either side and taking a breath. Don't actually take your head out of the water—turn it just enough so that it's out of the water to take a breath. Technically, you can breathe on both sides but it's much easier to stick to one side. Beginners should take a breath for each arm repetition. As your shoulder rises out of the water, rotate your head for a breath. Kicking too much will wind you. Relax your legs and use the down kick for balance and slight propulsion. Keep your fingers closed and cup your hands while reaching them out and pulling back in an "S" motion so that the hand comes out of the water at your side.

BREASTSTROKE

Another popular paddle, the breaststroke isn't as intense as the crawl. In fact, it's often used by lap swimmers as a cool-down stroke. Essentially, you're on your stomach while moving your arms out in front of you to their full length and pulling back to a point about even with your shoulders. Again, keep your fingers closed and cup the hands. The kick for this one is a scissor-kick motion, which happens at the same time as your arm stroke. Each time you stroke and kick lift your mouth out of the water and take a breathe as you look forward.

DID YOU KNOW?

Lynne Cox has become an American icon for her "open water swimming." She became the fastest person to cross the English Channel in 1972. In later years she crossed the Cook Straits in New Zealand and the Straits of Magellan in Chile and swam around Cape Point in Africa, never mind the sharks or near freezing water temperature. Her most famous swim was in 1987 when she swam the Bering Strait from Alaska to Russia at the height of the Cold War. Most recently she swam a mile along the coastline of Antarctica in water that was a couple of degrees BELOW freezing.

BODY SURFING

Body surfing—literally using your body like a surfboard so that the motion of the wave carries you forward along with it—is a blast and anyone can do it. After a little practice you'll even be able to guide your way back and forth and over the top of your temporary people mover.

SKILL LEVEL	● ●
TIME NEEDED	1–2 hours

You don't need any equipment and it's most fun to do close to the beach. However, you do have to be careful not to get caught in a big breaker. Those can bang you up pretty good on the ocean floor. And just forget body surfing anywhere near coral. You're just asking for trouble on that one.

YOU WILL NEED

Waves

Flippers (optional)

1 Like surfing, get to a place in the water where you're just past where the waves are breaking.

2 When you see a wave you want to catch, start swimming toward the beach until the wave catches you before it breaks. You might want to wear flippers so that you can swim a little faster.

3 Waves break either left or right, and it's obvious which way (usually, they'll be breaking the same way all day long). When you start to feel yourself carried along by a wave head away from the part of the wave that's breaking. Stop using your arms, keep kicking, and use the palms of your hands to balance yourself on the top of the water.

4 When you start to get to the end of your ride or you feel the wave about to crash on the beach, pull your body up so that the top of the wave washes over your back.

JELLYFISH

When swimming in the ocean, keep in mind the creatures that live in the ocean. One critter you definitely want to stay away from is the jellyfish. The good thing is that they're not out to get you. They just float. But that's also the bad thing. While they're floating around, you could swim into them and get stung by their long, almost invisible tentacles. These launch barbed stingers and poison that can go straight through your skin. It hurts like you know what. In short, avoid jellyfish. Usually lifeguards put up signs at the beach if there are jellyfish in the water. If you do get stung, the lifeguards will also have some medicine on hand. If there are no lifeguards, use vinegar, meat tenderizer, or rubbing alcohol on a jellyfish sting to get rid of the pain.

SURFING

There's nothing like the feeling of catching the perfect wave. The sound of the ocean, the sea breeze in your face as you glide along a wave. Surfing is the very definition of freedom. And like freedom it takes some practice to find a groove. Beginners should forget the North Shore of Hawaii. Go for the equivalent of the Bunny Slopes and stick to the 3-foot high waves. They'll be a lot more fun than the mountains of water the pros risk their necks on anyway. Also, check with the local surf shops to find a good location to match your experience level. Consider lessons. What you don't want to do is just drop in to some deserted beach. As with any ocean swimming, you have to watch for rip tides. Surfers should also know where underwater rocks and corals are. Here are some pointers to get you started:

SKILL LEVEL	● ● ●
TIME NEEDED	1½–2 hours

YOU WILL NEED

A waxed surfboard between 7 and 8 ft (2 and 2.5 m) long

Sunscreen

Waves about 3 ft (1 m) high

1 Before getting in the water, put your board flat on the sand and stand on it with one foot forward and one foot back. Whatever foot you naturally place toward the back of the board is your back foot and that's the one you want to attach the ankle leash to.

2 To get out to where the waves are, wait until a wave breaks on shore and then run into the water and do a kind of belly flop on your board, which should send you gliding out into the surf.

3 Lie on the center of the board (lying too far forward will cause the nose of the board to dip in the water when you're paddling out to the waves or when you're paddling to catch a wave and that will hinder your progress). Paddle in strong, even strokes.

4 When you come to a wave that threatens to crash on top of you, do a "duck dive" by dipping the nose of the surfboard into the water and ducking your head in with it so that you go under the water (and the break) and pop up on the other side of the wave like a duck hunting for fish. This takes good timing and a fair bit of practice.

5 Paddle out to an area just past where the waves are breaking, sit up on your board, and wait.

6 When a rideable wave approaches, turn your board toward shore and paddle strongly until you feel the wave start to propel you forward.

7 Grab the sides or "rails" of the board with both hands and do a quick push up while bringing your feet underneath you, so that you end up in a squatting position with one foot in front of the other and your toes pointed toward the board's center stripe. You should still be holding onto the rails.

8 Let go of the rails and stand up, keeping your knees bent and your arms away from your body for balance.

9 Once you're up, simply follow the direction that the wave is breaking in. Keep the nose and the tail of the board from dipping too far in the water by moving your feet either to the front or the back. Control the side-to-side direction of the board by leaning in the direction you want to go.

BEWARE OF THE SHARKS!

To be totally honest, sharks are pretty low on the list of things you need to watch out for in the ocean. Getting attacked by a shark is very rare—one statistic says that there are 75 shark attacks a year WORLDWIDE, only 10 of which result in deaths. Still, they're out there, and there are some precautions you can take to avoid becoming shark food:

Check if sharks are common in the areas you are swimming in.

Stay out of the water if you're bleeding because sharks can smell and taste blood in the water, like a trail of breadcrumbs leading right to you.

Don't swim where there are lots of fishermen tossing bait fish into the water.

WAVE JUMPING

You can still have fun in the waves, even if you don't fancy surfing or bodysurfing, from bobbing up and over them, to diving straight into them and harmlessly out the other side as the tops break over and past you. It's even fun trying to jump over a wave and having the curling lip hit you in the legs and flip your body over. If you're going to try that, timing is everything.

Most waves occur because of distant winds that push the surface of the ocean. They can grow the farther they travel and they don't stop until they break on the beach. Waves that have traveled a long way, with strong and consistent winds out at sea, can be really huge and these are good for surfing.

You don't really want to swim in waves over, say, 5 feet (1.5 m) high. If these break on top of you they can push you down to the seabed and drag you along helplessly. Best to stick to the smaller ones and only swim where there's a sandy bottom instead of a coral bottom, which can tear you up.

For smaller waves you might get a kick out of letting one crash on top of you, but even then you'll feel the awesome power of all that water and energy pushing you around. If the waves are dauntingly big, best to treat a day of swimming with the waves as a game of keep away—you trying to keep away from the break of the white water.

ROWING A BOAT

Rowboats are a great way to have fun on the water with your family, and a lot of popular vacation places on lakes and rivers have rowboats you can rent for a few hours or even the whole day. If you've never rowed before, start off on quiet waters. And if you're on a river, remember to take the currents into account—if you start rowing downstream, it could be much harder work coming back!

1 Sit in your rowboat between the oarlocks, with your back facing the bow (the front of the boat). There may be foot braces at your feet for extra leverage.

2 Put the oars in the oarlocks, take hold of the handles, and place your feet in the braces. Position the oars a little above the water, making sure that the oar blade is perpendicular to the surface.

3 Now lean forward, slightly bending your knees, and extend your arms fully forward, so that the oar paddles are behind you.

4 Dip the oar blades into the water and begin the stroke by slightly extending your legs.

5 Use your back and torso to carry the oars through the water, keeping your arms straight until you're sitting upright in the seat.

6 To finish the stroke, bring your arms into your chest. The stroke should be a fluid movement that includes legs, back, and arms.

SKILL LEVEL

TIME NEEDED 1 hour

YOU WILL NEED

A rowboat

Oars

DID YOU KNOW?

Nothing matches the fierce competitiveness of college rowing. In one style of boat race, called "bumps," teams chase each other, trying to bump into the boat in front without getting bumped by the boat behind. Legend has it that, in 1876, one of the teams in a college race in Cambridge, England, tied a sword to their boat to try to sink an opposing team. Unfortunately, instead of poking a hole in the boat they ended up poking a hole in the helmsman! They were disqualified from racing ever again.

WATERSKIING

Waterskiing is either a boatload of fun or it's not. If you fall and swallow a gallon of water on the way down, it can be discouraging.

SKILL LEVEL	●●●
TIME NEEDED	1–2 hours

YOU WILL NEED

A boat

A boat driver

Water skis

A life jacket

1 Get in the water and hold onto the handle of the rope attached to the boat. Float upright with the tips of your skis out of the water about a foot apart, with the ski rope between them.

2 Bend your knees as if you were in a crouch position or sitting in a chair in the water.

3 Give the driver a signal to start. When you start to feel the rope go tense, lean back slightly (but not too much) and straighten your back.

4 Keep your knees bent and let the boat pull you up out of the water.

5 Once you're up, stay inside the boat's wake until you feel comfortable enough to venture outside it. If you don't manage to stay up the first time, don't get discouraged, just keep trying.

BURYING DAD IN THE SAND

It's fun to bury dad or big brother in the sand—hopefully you'll have a willing volunteer among your family or friends. At least once they're buried, they don't have to worry about getting a sunburn.

SKILL LEVEL	●
TIME NEEDED	½ hour

YOU WILL NEED

A good site near wet sand but not so close to the sea that high tide is going to wash you away

Shovel, scoop, or hands

1 First, dig a trench into which a person can fit comfortably, with their head out at one end. The trench should be at least a foot deep, probably more. Pile all the sand from the pit around its edges.

2 Next, get your volunteer to lie down in the pit and wriggle his body into position so that the sand fits to the contours of his body.

3 Now start pushing the sand over his body until he's completely buried.

4 Once you have buried your volunteer, you can draw or build new body shapes out of the sand above him—dad's head, with the body of a fish! Don't forget to dig him out before you leave.

SNORKELING

Jumping into the water with a mask, snorkel, and fins is one of the most exciting ways to explore the underwater world. Just like walking through a forest or a trek through the mountains, snorkeling brings discoveries the likes of which you rarely see. Get ready to find colorful corals, unusual fish, and a vast array of plant and marine life.

SKILL LEVEL ◉ ◉

TIME NEEDED 1–2 hours

EQUIPMENT The key to a fun snorkeling session is a combination of having the right equipment and the right location. The equipment is easy enough to find, but there are cheap snorkeling sets that might do well enough in a pool but won't hold up to the ocean. The mask is the most important piece of a snorkeler's equipment. It should cover your nose and form a seal against your face to keep the water out. Check to see that it fits by placing it on your fact and sucking in through your nose. If it sticks, it's a good fit. Fins are also important because they allow you to swim against ocean currents and cover more distance that you'd be able to without them. The best fins are the ones that completely cover your heel, rather than the ones that have a strap only across the back.

The snorkel itself fits into rubber rings on the side of the mask or it can just go between the strap and your head. Position it so it fits in your mouth comfortably. Water often gets inside the snorkel so you should practice clearing it out by blasting the water out with a burst of air. Obviously you can't breathe in before you blast, so use your diaphragm and stomach muscles to force the water out. This takes some practice. Don't get discouraged if you have to stop, take the snorkel out of your mouth and dump the water out that way.

YOU WILL NEED

A mask

A snorkel

A pair of flippers

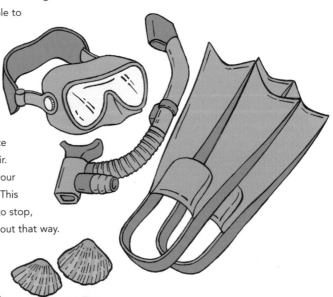

BEFORE YOU JUMP IN If you've never snorkeled before, your first shot at it should be in calm water over shallow reefs. Protected lagoons are perfect. Open water can have waves that could unsettle you. But even before you get into the water, strap on the gear and have a practice in the pool so that you can get used to breathing through the snorkel. Rub saliva on the lens of your mask and then rinse it to prevent the mask from fogging up. When you put it on, make sure there are no stray hairs under the rubber rim and place the head strap in a way that won't pull hair or pinch ears.

When you're ready to get in the water, just be sure to ask around about currents. Never get in the water where a sign is posted about rip tides, strong currents that can carry you far out to sea. Once you find a calm clear spot, just follow the coral. Float on top of the water using your flippers to move around and just take in the undersea life—and you can dive down in deeper water to take a closer view if anything interesting catches your eye.

EXPLORING THE UNDERWATER WORLD

The flora and fauna found under the waves is as diverse as any found on land. What many people don't realize is that coral is alive. As it sways in the ocean currents, it may look like a plant, but it's actually an animal. Scientifically, coral is part of a phylum called Cnidaria and there are all kinds of colors, shapes, and sizes of coral with names like Brain, Leaf, and Tube. They live underwater, blanketing the surface of the rocks. Enormous patches of coral consist of hundreds and sometimes thousands of different species. Coral eat microscopic animals called zooplankton. You can see their mouths, which are surrounded by feathery stinging tentacles that trap the zooplankton.

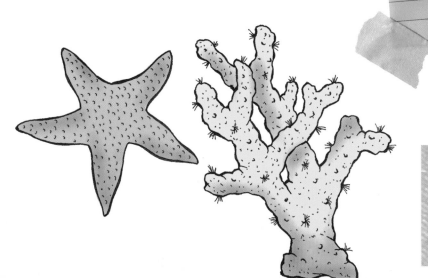

TOP TIP

Don't touch the coral! It's sharp and can easily cut you. Plus, it's a sensitive ecosystem that is easily damaged.

OUTDOORS

The first thing to do on a beautiful summer's
day is to get outside! The great outdoors offers
much more opportunity for summer fun and
adventure. Whether you stay in your own backyard
building a treehouse or investigating the insect
wildlife, or venture further afield to go hiking or
camping, there's always plenty to do. You can even
find out how to predict the weather, so you can avoid
getting caught in a downpour while you're out!

MAKE A KITE

Reach up to the skies with a homemade kite. This can be quite challenging so an extra pair of hands is probably a good idea. Make sure any decoration you add is even so that your kite stays balanced—if you have too much weight on one side, the kite will spin out of control when the wind blows and crash rather than fly.

SKILL LEVEL ◉ ◉

TIME NEEDED 45 minutes

1 Cut thin, shallow notches in the ends of both pieces of cane. These notches don't have to be thicker than the blade of the knife.

2 Make a cross by placing the shorter piece of cane over the longer piece. They should intersect about 1 foot (30 cm) down on the longer piece.

3 Secure them in place by lashing them with thick twine. Pass the twine around the crossing point in an "X," and tuck the end under the loops to finish off.

4 Now make a tight frame of twine around the canes, using the notches you made in step 1 as guides. First make a loop in the end of the twine, using a bowline knot. Lodge the knot on one notch (so the loop hangs free the other side) and stretch the string all the way around, passing through each notch until you come back to the loop.

5 Pass the twine through the loop and stretch it back around the frame in the reverse direction. Repeat steps 4 and 5 a few times. This will make the twine frame taut. Be careful not to make it too tight or the canes will warp.

6 Lay the cane and twine frame over your sheet of paper. Trace around the kite frame onto the paper, giving yourself at least 1 inch (2.5 cm) extra paper all around the outline.

7 Cut the shape of the kite out of the paper. Don't forget to make the paper a little larger than the kite. Attach the paper to the face of the cane kite frame by folding the extra width of paper over the twine all the way around, and taping it to the back.

8 Create the kite "harness" by tying a piece of twine at the top and bottom of the long piece of cane, and another piece at the ends of the shorter piece of cane. They

YOU WILL NEED

1 straight, thin piece of cane about 3 ft (90 cm) long

1 straight, thin piece of cane 18 in (45 cm) long

A good, long piece of thick twine

A long kite string

Scissors

A large piece of thick white paper, at least 3 x 1 ft (90 x 30 cm)

Masking tape

Ribbon

WARNING

Stay away from electrical lines. If your kite becomes entangled, leave it there. Never fly your kite during a thunderstorm.

should intersect about 6 inches (15 cm) above the intersection of the canes. Tie the two pieces of twine together at that point, and make a small twine loop in one of the tied ends. This is where you'll attach your kite string when you're ready to fly.

9 Make a kite tail with a 3-foot (90-cm) length of twine. Tie 4-inch (10-cm) pieces of ribbon to the twine every 6 inches (15 cm), or as you like.

10 Tie the kite string to the loop, and you're ready to take your kite outside on a windy day and launch!

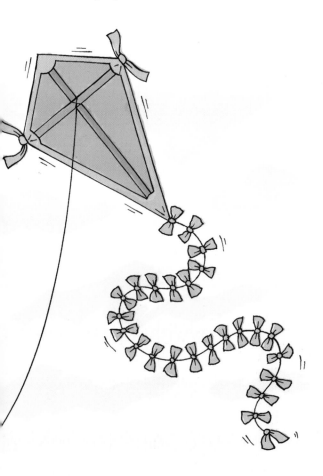

FLY A KITE

If there's a bit of a breeze outside, why not dig out your old kite (or make your own from the instructions opposite) and have some fun? There's nothing like feeling the live pull of a kite on the end of a string—just hold on tight so it doesn't fly away without you.

SKILL LEVEL	◉
TIME NEEDED	½ hour

YOU WILL NEED

A kite

A moderately windy day (too gusty and you'll lose your kite)

1 Find a large open area free of trees and electrical lines.

2 Let out a small length of kite string and, holding the string in your hand, run with the kite behind you into the wind until it lifts it.

3 Keep letting out string until the kite reaches a good height.

4 Keep an eye on your kite, in case the wind drops. Run into the wind or pull on the string to give your kite some extra lift.

5 Bring the kite down by slowly winding the kite string around the kite spool, and catch it just before it hits the ground to avoid damaging it.

BUILD A TREEHOUSE

Building a treehouse is always a great adventure. Once you've finished, it'll make a great lookout platform, fort, or base camp. Fit it out with pulleys, climbing ropes, and telescopes and you can spend hours exploring without even moving.

SKILL LEVEL	● ●
TIME NEEDED	1 day

1 Start by cutting 18-inch (45-cm) long pieces from your length of wood to make a basic ladder up the trunk of the tree. Pick the exact spot you want to build in, and work out how many rungs you'll need on your ladder to climb up to it.

2 Once the pieces have been cut, use at least two nails set side-by-side in each piece to nail the rungs to the tree. Space them about 2 feet (60 cm) apart, leading up the trunk to the base of the branches where the platform of the treehouse will be secured.

3 How you access the platform will depend on the shape of your tree. Most of the time, the ladder will come up right under the best branches for building on. That's fine. You'll just have to cut a hole in your floor to climb through. If you keep the piece of wood you cut out, you can use it to make a trap door.

4 Next, haul the sheet of plywood into the tree and position it between the branches where you think it will be most sturdy.

5 Mark the tree limbs with a pencil or nail where the plywood touches them and lower the plywood back down.

6 Cut several more 18-inch long pieces of wood and nail them to the tree at the spots you've marked to act as blocks for your platform.

7 Lift the plywood carefully into place by having two people on the ground pass it up to two people in the tree. Nail the plywood to the blocks.

8 Next, make railings by nailing up more lengths of plywood between the branches or by tying up pieces of rope to surround your platform.

9 From here you can add a trapdoor, extra ladder steps leading to higher branches, and miniature seats or platforms on surrounding lookout points.

YOU WILL NEED

A suitable tree (see below)

A hammer

Rope

Sturdy length of wood and thick plywood base

A saw (you will need an adult's help to use this)

A ladder

Galvanized nails

TOP TIP

Choose a sturdy tree with a minimum of three branches that spread out equal distances from one side of the trunk. They should be at least 8 inches (20 cm) thick to support the weight of you and a few friends. Don't build as high as you can: a treehouse platform acts like a sail when it's windy and it can sway around a lot. Better to aim for between 10 and 15 feet (3 and 4.5 m) off the ground. That'll feel quite high enough when there's a strong breeze!

READING A MAP

There's no greater sense of freedom than setting off on a day's adventure with your friends, armed only with a packed lunch and a map. But before you head off into the wild blue yonder, there are a few basic skills that you should get under your belt, like how to read a map.

SKILL LEVEL   ● ●

TIME NEEDED   1–2 hours

1 Find somewhere on the map that you want to travel to, and make sure you know what your current position is on the map.

YOU WILL NEED

A full-color map

A compass

5 As you're walking, take note of your natural surroundings, like streams, buildings, and areas of woodland. Then check to make sure they're on the map too by referring to the key, so you know you're on the right track. Don't forget to take regular bearings during your journey to also help keep you on track.

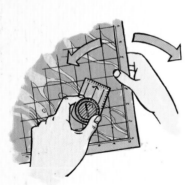

arrow aligns itself with the compass's magnetic needle. This sets your bearing into the compass.

2 Put your compass on the map and line up the sides of the compass base plate with an imaginary line going from your present location to your destination. This means the direction arrow at the top of the compass base plate should be pointing in the direction of your destination

3 Without moving the compass base plate, rotate the central dial in the middle until its north

4 To reach your destination walk in the direction of the arrow on the base plate while ensuring that the magnetic needle is aligned with the north arrow on the compass.

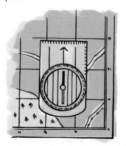

TOP TIP

Check the scale on the map when you plan your route—a 1:50,000 map scale means the map area is 50,000 times smaller than the real area, so a distance of 1 inch (2.5 cm) on the map is 50,000 inches (125,000 cm), or about 0.8 miles (1.25 km).

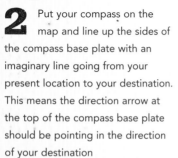

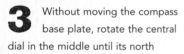

FINDING NORTH

If you're planning any long summer hikes, you'll need to be able to find your way around. You should always have a map and compass with you so that you don't get lost, but if you want to add an additional challenge to your expedition, try finding your way north without using your compass. Lots of adventurers in history didn't have any instruments at all and they managed to complete their missions. You can too! You can find north using a few different methods without a compass.

SKILL LEVEL	◉
TIME NEEDED	5 minutes

USING A WATCH

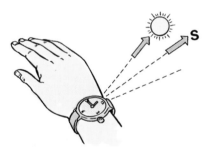

A watch can be made into a compass. Just hold it horizontal to the ground and point the hour hand directly at the sun. Then imagine a line running exactly in the middle between the hour hand and the 12 o'clock mark on your watch. That imaginary line points north and south—south being at the top of the line, which usually means you'll be facing south with north behind you.

If you're in the southern hemisphere point the watch's 12 o'clock mark in the direction of the sun and your north/south line will run between this and wherever the hour hand is. In this case, north is at the top of this line, meaning you'll probably be facing north with the southerly direction behind you.

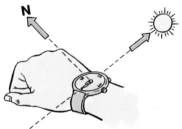

If you have a digital watch, no problem! Draw out a watch with hands showing the right time on paper. Then follow the previous steps using the clock you have drawn.

YOU WILL NEED

A watch

USING SHADOW STICKS

Another method for finding directions is by reading shadows. It's pretty easy, but you'll need at least 15 minutes to discover which way is north.

1 Find a straight, good-sized stick, about 3 feet (90 cm) long, and plant it so it stands up straight in level ground where it can cast a clear shadow.

2 Mark the tip of its shadow with one of your two stones. This will be your west mark.

3 Wait at least 15 minutes, then go back and check the shadow's progress—it will have moved.

4 Now mark the new shadow tip with your other stone and you will have an east mark.

5 Draw a line between the two marks for a west/east line. Draw another line exactly perpendicular to this one to form a north/south line.

6 By placing your left foot at the west mark and your right foot at the east mark you will always be facing north. This rule applies anywhere in the world.

SKILL LEVEL	☀
TIME NEEDED	5 minutes

YOU WILL NEED

A stick

2 stones

USING THE STARS

The ancient Polynesians of the South Pacific may have been history's best navigators. They discovered and settled thousands of islands without any instruments at all—only the knowledge of the sky that was passed down the generations through stories. Polynesian navigators, or palus, were required to train for a long time before they could navigate their own ships. One part of the training was memorizing the colors of the sky and sea, the various clouds that would cluster over islands, and the stars. Here's how to follow their example.

SKILL LEVEL	●
TIME NEEDED	5 minutes

YOU WILL NEED

A clear, starry night

NORTHERN HEMISPHERE

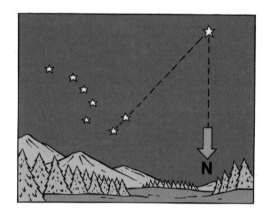

1 Find the North Star, usually one of the brightest in the night sky, by first locating the Big Dipper. Draw an imaginary line joining the two stars that form the Big Dipper's front line, and continue this line out about five times its original length. You should arrive at the North Star.

2 Now just draw an imaginary line from the North Star down to Earth. The star sits directly over the North Pole, so that way is north.

SOUTHERN HEMISPHERE

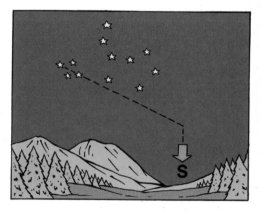

1 There is no North Star in the southern hemisphere. Instead, locate the constellation known as the Southern Cross, next to the constellation Centaurus.

2 Once you've picked out the four bright stars that form the Cross, look to the two stars that make the longer of the two crossbeams.

3 Extend this crossbeam out to five times its length and mark that imaginary point in the sky. A line drawn from that point down to Earth will give you an approximate south reading.

STARGAZING

Stargazing has been a human pastime for as long as there have been humans. Tracking the movements of constellations (groups of stars) was a way to mark the seasons for the Ancient Egyptians back in 2000 B.C. The Mesopotamians, in 1000 B.C. began to map the night sky in more detail. Then a Greek man named Ptolemy, who lived in Roman Egypt, was the first to name what we in the Western world know as the constellations. Some of our Solar System's planets are even visible to the naked eye—see if you can spot them.

SPOTTING PLANETS

There are five planets that are visible to the naked eye—Mercury, Venus, Mars, Jupiter, and Saturn. Astronomers in the past called these bright lights in the sky "wandering stars," because they moved across the sky in different directions and at different speeds than the stars that make up the constellations. In fact "planet" in Greek means "wanderer."

The planets are named after the Roman gods and were long ago thought to be actual living creatures. With the addition of the sun and the moon, the names of the planets (translated from Latin to Anglo-Saxon) gave us the seven days of the week. In China and Japan, the five planets are named after the five elements: Mercury is the water star, Venus is the metal star, Mars is the fire star, Jupiter is the wood star and Saturn is the earth star.

MERCURY You can only see Mercury in the early morning or late afternoon, just before the sun comes up or just after it goes down. Look for Mercury in the direction of the sunset about 45 minutes after the sun dips beneath the horizon, or in the direction of sunrise about 45 minutes before the sun comes up. The best times for viewing in the northern hemisphere are March and April (during sunset) and September and October (during sunrise). The opposite is true if you're planet-spotting in the southern hemisphere, where the best times to spot Mercury are sunrise in March and April, and sunset in September and October.

VENUS Venus is always the third-brightest object in the sky after the sun and moon, and is known alternately as the Morning or Evening Star. Venus can also be seen by looking in the direction of the setting or rising sun, and it is visible for much longer periods of time than Mercury.

MARS Mars is visible all night and is brightest every two years, when its orbit is closest to the Earth's and it is in opposition to our planet (the Earth is between it and the sun). The planet follows the same path as the sun across the night sky and is most visible looking east in the early morning. You can recognize it by its orange-red color.

JUPITER Even though it's much further away, Jupiter is the next brightest object in the sky after Venus because it's so large—1,300 times the volume of the Earth! Like Venus, it is best seen during twilight hours. Those with a telescope might be able to see Jupiter's large red spot, which is actually a colossal storm twice the size of Earth.

SATURN Because Saturn is so far away (10 times further away from the sun than Earth), it's hard to see unless you know where to look. It's at its brightest when its rings are fully facing the Earth, but that last happened in 2002 and won't happen again until 2017. For now, look for a pale yellow star low in the western sky around dusk.

URANUS, NEPTUNE, AND PLUTO The three outermost planets in the Solar System are hard to see without a telescope. Pluto is now actually classified as a dwarf planet, much smaller than the others in the Solar System, and impossible to see with the naked eye.

CONSTELLATIONS

There are actually 88 different constellations mapped out all across the sky from Pole to Pole, east and west. The constellations you can see are different in the northern and southern hemispheres, because the curve of the Earth hides some stars from us. You can look up star charts on the Internet or your local library, which will tell you exactly where to look for constellations in different places and at different times of year. They can also tell you when to look for exciting events like meteor showers or a lunar eclipse! It's best to do your star-spotting away from cities, though. Light pollution from streetlights in urban areas makes it hard to see faint objects in the skies.

THE ZODIAC AND ASTROLOGY

The constellations of the zodiac can be found roughly along the path that the sun takes across the sky. They have been identified and studied by human civilizations for thousands of years. They are called: Aries (the ram), Taurus (the bull), Gemini (the twins), Cancer (the crab), Leo (the lion), Virgo (the virgin), Libra (the scales), Scorpio (the scorpion), Sagittarius (the archer), Capricorn (the goat), Aquarius (the water-bearer), and Pisces (the fish). Each one has its own meanings and symbol. They are the basis for astrology, a system that many people believe can predict the future by the movements of the stars. Each symbol is most visible at a particular time of year, and people born during that time are said to have characteristics of that symbol. Find your birthday on the list to see what star sign you are.

SIGNS OF THE ZODIAC

Aries: 21 March–20 April

Taurus: 21 April–21 May

Gemini: 22 May–21 June

Cancer: 22 June–23 July

Leo: 24 July–23 August

Virgo: 24 August–23 September

Libra: 24 September–23 October

Scorpio: 24 October–22 November

Sagittarius: 23 November–22 December

Capricorn: 23 December–20 January

Aquarius: 21 January–19 February

Pisces: 20 February–20 March

MODELING THE SOLAR SYSTEM

It's one thing to know that the Earth is 93 million miles (150 million km) from the sun, and Neptune is 2.7 billion miles (4.3 billion km) from the Earth at its closest point. But, what exactly would that look like? Here's a hint: it's a very, very long way. But with numbers that large, it's impossible to get a picture of it in your mind. Here's how to use a roll of toilet paper to help you comprehend the enormous distances between the planets. You'll need a fair amount of space for this, so it's best to do it outside if possible, and if the weather isn't too windy. However, if you do have an indoor room or hallway long enough, you can put it together inside as well.

SKILL LEVEL　　　　　　　　●

TIME NEEDED　　　　　　½ hour

1 Starting at one end of your chosen space, unroll the first sheet of toilet paper and tape it to the floor to hold it in place.

2 Make a dot on the perforation between the first and second sheets (the dot should be about half the size of the end of a pencil). Label it "Sun." At the scale we're using to map out our paper Solar System, this dot is an accurate representation of the size of the sun. At this scale, the rest of the planets in the solar system would be too small to see, so mark them with "X."

YOU WILL NEED

A roll of toilet paper with 200 sheets per roll

An outside area (or room or hallway) long enough to unroll the entire roll of toilet paper

10 different-colored markers

Clear tape

3 Now unroll 10 sheets of paper and label all of the planets in their correct order, marking "X"es on the paper in the following order: 2 sheets from the sun is Mercury; 3.7 sheets from the sun is Venus; 5.1 sheets from the sun is Earth; and then 7.7 sheets from the sun is Mars.

4 Now unroll all 200 sheets of the toilet paper, and mark on the remaining planets: Jupiter is 26.4 sheets from the sun, Saturn is 48.4 sheets from the sun, Uranus is 97.3 sheets, and Neptune is at 152.4 sheets. Pluto, though it's technically not a planet, is exactly 200 sheets of toilet paper away.

Now you've seen how huge the distances are between the planets, you can understand how difficult it is for human beings to travel to even our closest neighbors. Although Venus is the planet closest to us, its hostile atmosphere would make it pretty dangerous for any humans to visit. We're much more likely to travel to Mars, which is farther away but has a more similar atmosphere and temperature to our own planet.

Still, it's not an easy journey—it takes 18 months for a spacecraft from Earth to travel to Mars, and any humans on board would have to carry enough food, air, and water to last them for a minimum of three years, and enough fuel to get there and back. One way around the problem would be to equip a spacecraft with gardens to produce food and oxygen to keep the astronauts alive on their journey. This would need an enormous spaceship, which would be too big and fragile to lift off from Earth like a rocket or shuttle. Instead it might have to be built in orbit by construction crews based on a space station using materials shipped up from Earth in shuttles or unmanned rockets.

DID YOU KNOW?

There are lots of other things in our galaxy besides planets, including an asteroid belt (about 18 sheets from the sun), comets, and moons. An unmanned spacecraft named *Voyager 2* was launched from Earth in 1977 to fly past and take pictures of as many planets in the Solar System as possible. In 1989, it flew past Neptune. Today it is more than 7.5 billion miles (12 billion km) from Earth—more than twice the distance that Pluto is from the sun. *Voyager 2* still transmits weekly signals back to Earth. You can monitor its progress, and the progress of its sister spacecraft *Voyager 1*, even farther out in space, on the NASA website.

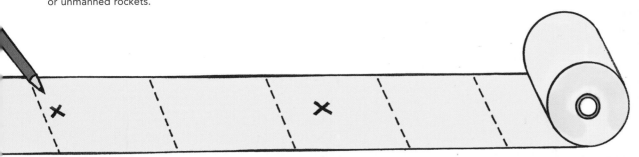

PREDICT THE WEATHER

Just because it's summer doesn't always mean it's going to be sunny. If you're planning an outdoors event like a picnic, or you've gone adventuring some distance from home, predicting the weather can be a very useful skill to have to avoid getting very wet. And it's also a good way to impress your fellow travelers.

CLOUD READING

There are four main types of clouds, and they are categorized depending on how high or low they float in the sky.

The highest floating clouds—16,500 ft (5 km) or higher—are in the cirrus family. Cirrus clouds are wispy and frozen and do not indicate bad weather.

Clouds floating in the middle range of the sky—6,500 to 16,500 ft (2 to 5 km) high—are known as alto clouds. They look like large patchy sheets that cover big parts of the sky. Seeing these on a warm day usually indicates thunderstorms later.

The lowest-floating clouds are stratus clouds. They can reach as high as 6,500 ft (2 km), but some stratus clouds drop all the way to the surface of the planet and are known as fog. While stratus clouds don't necessarily forecast rain, some of the types of clouds in this family do. Nimbostratus clouds,

for example, look gray and fluffy while covering the entire sky. Expect rain in the next few hours if you see these.

The last type of cloud is the vertical cloud, which can reach from ground level up to several kilometers high. These are the cumulus clouds, sometimes known as thunderheads. They are white, puffy, and massive, and, as their name indicates, they forecast thunder, lightning, and heavy rain or hail. If you see these rolling in, then watch out: a storm's brewing.

MAKING A WEATHER VANE

Another good method of predicting the weather is to know which way the wind is blowing, using a weather vane. Keep a log of the wind direction on rainy days and fine days and see if you can work out a pattern. If you know it always rains when the wind is in the southwest, you'll know what to expect the next time the wind blows from that direction.

SKILL LEVEL	◉ ◉
TIME NEEDED	5 minutes

YOU WILL NEED

A broom handle

A hammer and a 3-in (7.5-cm) nail

A saw (ask an adult for help to use this)

A 12-in (30-cm) piece of wood

Scrap pieces of plywood

Wood glue

1 Cut two pieces of plywood to make a triangle and a rectangle. Cut slits at each end of your piece of wood, and glue the plywood shapes into the slits to make a wooden arrow.

2 Hammer the nail through the center of your arrow. Turn the nail a few times until the hole loosens so the arrow can spin freely.

3 Hammer the rest of the nail into the broom handle. Plant it securely in the ground in a windy spot and use a compass to tell which direction the arrow is pointing—that's where the wind is coming from!

INSECT HUNTING

Finding insects isn't hard—there are over one million species of insect in the world, from beetles, bees, and ants to grasshoppers, butterflies, and praying mantises. And summer is the best time to look for them.

SKILL LEVEL	◉
TIME NEEDED	½ hour

YOU WILL NEED

A glass jar with a lid

A piece of cardboard

A magnifying glass

A pencil and notebook

1 Start by looking under rocks, in soil, and in damp, shady areas.

2 Once you find an insect you like, gently pick it up (using the cardboard if you don't want to touch it), drop it in the jar and put the lid on.

3 Sketch the insect and take notes. Compare your notes later with an encyclopedia or Internet guide to find out more. Then let the insect go—it needs the great outdoors to survive.

WARNING!

Don't forget that some insects, like ants, wasps, bees and scorpions, can give nasty bites or stings.

MAKING A TENT

You won't need to make a huge tent—
let's just focus on keeping the rain off
you and your friends. Once you get the
tent up, collect pine needles, dried
leaves, grass, and other soft things to
make a natural floor.

SKILL LEVEL	● ●
TIME NEEDED	1–2 hours

YOU WILL NEED

A 8- x 12-ft (2.4- x 3.6-m) tarpaulin with
grommets (eyelets) around the edges

24-ft (7-m) rope

At least four large rocks or stakes

1 Locate two trees about 10 ft (3 m) apart.
These will act as the supports for your tent.

2 Run your rope through the center grommet on
each of the longer sides of the tarpaulin,
bisecting it into 6- x 8-ft (1.3- x 2.4-m) rectangles.

3 About 5 ft (1.5 m) off the ground, securely tie
the rope to the trees at roughly the same
height on each tree. The tarpaulin should drape
over this roof-line.

4 Use rocks or stakes to secure the corners of
the tarpaulin, stretching the sides of your
tent taut.

BIRD-WATCHING

Birds are fascinating creatures: from
hummingbirds to eagles, they come in
every color of the rainbow and are found
on every continent. Bird-watching can
be a challenge, both because they're hard
to get close to and because they're often
well-camouflaged. Here are a few tips
on how to spot and identify them.

SKILL LEVEL	● ●
TIME NEEDED	1–2 hours

YOU WILL NEED

A pair of good binoculars

A guide to birds in your region

A pad and pencil

1 Get your equipment and head somewhere near
water, or a food source like trees with fruit or
berries, where birds naturally congregate.

2 Either set up a hideout (see page 55) or find
somewhere sheltered to wait quietly.

3 When you spot an interesting bird, train the
binoculars on it. Make notes about its size,
the shape of its beak, any markings around the
head and chest, and the shape of its tail feathers.

4 Like all animals, different birds are found in
different regions. Use your guide to identify
what you've seen from your notes.

TRACKING

Your local wildlife will probably be most abundant in summer, when all the animals are out of their winter hibernation and their young are emerging from their nests and dens, so there should be plenty of tracks for you to find. Find out which animals live in your area, and what you can expect to see (and what you should avoid). Tracking animals and birds requires a powerful sense of awareness and observation. There are footprints to recognize, but that's the easy part. Skilled trackers also know how to find and follow all kinds of signs, symbols, and clues, such as fur or feathers, broken sticks and leaves, and animal scents and dung.

SKILL LEVEL	● ●
TIME NEEDED	1–2 hours

DID YOU KNOW?

Dinosaur footprints from millions of years ago have been preserved as fossils. These fossils, called "ichnites," tell us about the way different dinosaurs moved around.

ANIMAL PRINTS

If you discover animal tracks, you'll want to know what kind of animal you're up against. Bears and large cats spell danger not adventure, so don't start following the trail if you spot their tracks. Deer, rabbits, foxes, and other small furry creatures are mostly harmless, and it can be good fun to track them back to their lair.

Wild dogs like foxes and wolves always have diamond-shaped paws that are longer than they are wide. Plus, they have four toes tipped by claw marks. Big cats, on the other hand, have retractable claws that won't show up in the mud (they also have four toes). Another characteristic of the big cats, like lions or jaguars, is that their toe marks are more circular than those of dogs. Bear prints have five toes with claw marks. They're also going to be significantly bigger than those of a fox or wildcat. Look across the page for some sample tracks.

HOW TO TRACK

Animals often use the same routes over and over, even if their territory covers hundreds of square miles. This makes things easier for the tracker—if you spot a well-used path, you can follow it to pick up the animal's trail. Of course, if the animal knows you're there they'll likely change course or hide. That's why tracking takes plenty of practice and patience.

Scientists have been tracking the movements of birds and animals for centuries, and even they've had to learn on the job. In the old days, scientists would tie string markers to the legs of migrating birds to see if they would return to the same spot a year later (they often did). Now scientists attach radio tags to all kinds of animals—from elephants and big cats to whales and dolphins—to track their movements all over the world by satellite.

Since most of us don't have access to electronic tags or satellites, we'll have to track like the primitive hunters in the old days. To follow an animal's trail, walk next to its prints, keeping the tracks between you and the sun so your shadow doesn't obscure them. Sometimes tracks can become faint, especially in drier weather, so try to spot

additional signs like broken foliage, flattened grass, or dung. Stay as quiet as you can. Talk in a whisper and avoid walking on dry twigs or leaves. Lastly, try to think like an animal—if you lose the trail in a natural boundary like a river or gorge, look for the easiest natural way forward. Follow your instincts until you catch up with the tracks again.

Often the tracks will stop at a burrow or watering place—if you wait there quietly (especially at dusk) there's a good chance you'll see your animal when it wakes up or decides it wants a drink. If you're lucky, and move quietly enough while you're tracking, you might catch up with whatever you're following, especially if it's stopping to graze or drink along the way. Then you can take a photo or just admire the creature—the best moment for any tracker.

FOOTPRINT PLASTER CASTS

Naturalists and other explorers use plaster casts as a way to gather facts. They can record and study fossils, footprints, leaves, bones, and other items found on their adventures by mixing up a simple recipe wherever they are. It's a lot easier than digging the whole thing out and dragging it back to the lab! If you're interested in nature, you can use plaster of paris to make a permanent record of any interesting tracks you find. Or, if you're lucky enough to dig up something exciting like a fossil, you can use the same technique to make copies for your friends.

SKILL LEVEL	
TIME NEEDED	1½ hours

1 Find an animal footprint—if you can't find an animal print, practice by making a print with your own foot.

2 Mix two cups (500 ml) of water with three cups (750 ml) of plaster of paris, adding the water a little at a time as you stir the mixture so you don't get lumps.

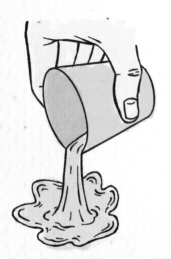

3 Pour the liquid plaster mix right into the print until it overflows a little at the top.

4 Leave the plaster to dry for an hour, then pull it up, wash off the soil, and you'll have an exact match of the print you found!

5 If you want to make a cast of an interesting leaf or shell that you've found, get a jar or two of putty, roll it out into a thick pancake, and then press your discovery into it. Once you get a good impression, mix up your plaster and pour it into the putty as you would have into the soil on the trail.

YOU WILL NEED

An animal footprint

Water

Dry plaster of paris

A plastic cup

Putty (optional)

2 cups (500 ml) of water

WARNING!

Plaster of paris undergoes a chemical reaction with water as it hardens, which gives out a lot of heat. Never attempt to make plaster casts of your hands or feet, or any other body part, as you can suffer severe burns inside the plaster as it sets.

BUILD A HIDEOUT

You can use a hideout to watch for animals and birds. Or you can keep it as base camp for your adventures, and as a place to store your adventuring supplies. Wherever you decide to build, seclusion is the key to a good hideout. It should be somewhere less traveled and not easily seen by the casual passerby.

SKILL LEVEL	◉
TIME NEEDED	1 hour

FINDING A SITE You can set up your hideout anywhere you want—even inside, perhaps up in the attic, if a rainy day interrupts your summer fun. Anywhere will do as long as you can find somewhere secluded. You could build one behind the shrubbery beside your house, in a wood thicket, inside a thick patch of bushes, or in a hollow tree in the woods.

CHOOSING YOUR MATERIALS All manner of materials can be used to construct a hideout, depending on where you want to build it. If you're outdoors and want to be protected from the elements, try stringing up a tarpaulin between two trees. If you don't expect to see much rain, cardboard could be your material of choice. A collection of large boxes can be linked together with tape, and you can cut out doors and windows. Use your imagination—anything that can be used to create a sense of private space will do.

HIDEOUT SUPPLIES Depending on its size, you may want to install some basic furniture in your shelter—old cable spools make great tables. Rocks or wooden boxes can be chairs. A cooler may also come in handy—it can double as a chair and you can store any provisions in it that you need for a day of adventuring.

WATCHING FOR WILDLIFE Hideouts are a good way to conceal yourself if you're watching for birds or animals. Many species will be scared off by the sight of a human being, so making a hideout among the natural vegetation will increase your chances of seeing something. Choose somewhere you know the animal or bird you're waiting to see likes to go, construct your hideout, then climb inside and wait quietly to see what comes along.

TOP TIP

You may need to add some extra camouflage to your hideout if you don't want it to be discovered by anyone else when you're not there, or if you want it better disguised when watching for the local wildlife. A few well-placed limbs from a nearby tree or bush will cover up your structure nicely.

SPORTS AND GAMES

Whether it's games in your own backyard, at the park, or at the pool, summer is the perfect time for getting active outside, and you'll find plenty of tips in the following chapter for old favorites as well as great new ideas. Try out silly games like the egg and spoon race and the three-legged race, test your skill at French bowls, hone your hula hoop technique, or team up for dodgeball. Whether you want a fun and silly game to keep you entertained or one with a bit of competition, there are plenty of options to try.

HOOPS

If you've never played hoops before, you've missed out on one of the fastest, high-energy, high-fun basketball games ever. It can be played on a court or just for fun with friends on the drive or in the backyard—wherever you can set up a hoop.

SKILL LEVEL	◉ ◉
TIME NEEDED	½ hour

1 Pick your teams. Flip a coin to see which team gets the ball first. The team with the ball first will throw in the ball from behind the 3-point line (a curved box running from the baseline rather like a penalty box in soccer).

2 The aim is to try to make a basket and to prevent the opposing team from doing the same. Each basket scored from inside the 3-point arc is worth a point, and each scored from behind the arc is worth 2 points. Most games are played to 20, although you can agree among yourselves.

3 After each made basket, the ball changes possession and is thrown in from behind the 3-point line. You also reset play in this way after an opposing team's missed basket or a steal—and you cannot reshoot a missed basket by the opposing team without resetting the play.

4 Throughout the game, you call your own fouls. These must be called as they happen. (Points do count if a player is fouled and the ball goes in the hoop. The first eight fouls are a reset of possession. Every foul after eight is a free throw, worth a point.)

5 Got all that? Well, let's shoot some hoops.

YOU WILL NEED

A basketball net

An area large enough to draw half a basketball court

6 players

BEAN BAG TOSS

Depending on where you were born and raised, you might call this game anything from corn toss to soft horseshoes. It doesn't much matter where you play or what you call it, it's good fun for all ages and can be played anywhere.

SKILL LEVEL	◉
TIME NEEDED	½ hour

YOU WILL NEED

2 bean bag or cornhole platforms (available from toy stores)

8 bean or corn bags

A minimum of 2 players

1 The bean bag platforms (wooden boxes with a large hole cut in top) are set about 30 feet (9 m) away from players.

2 Divide players into teams. A player from each team takes a turn to pitch his/her four bean bags at the bean bag platforms until a contestant reaches the score of 21 points. A bean bag in the hole scores 3 points, while one on the platform scores 1 point.

3 You'll be surprised at how the scoring whizzes along and how often the lead can change hands before a winner is declared.

HULA HOOP

Most famous as the big fitness fad of the 1950s, the hula hoop is making a popular comeback in playgrounds and backyards everywhere—and not just with the kids. Watch grandma relive her youth as she gives it a whirl as well.

SKILL LEVEL	◉
TIME NEEDED	5 minutes

YOU WILL NEED

A plastic hula hoop

1 Hold the hula hoop at waist height. Using both arms, swing the hoop around your waist to get it moving.

2 Keep it moving by gyrating your hips—you'll soon get the hang of it with a bit of practice.

TOP TIP

There are lots of competitions you can have with your friends involving hula hoops. For example, you could see who can do the most complete circles, who can hula hoop the longest or do the most hula hoops at one time, or who can run the furthest while hula hooping.

TUG-OF-WAR

You need plenty of muscle on your side to succeed at tug-of-war, but there's a surprising amount of technique involved too. In fact, brains and brawn are the ideal combination for this game that was originally played by British sailors on their long voyages around the world.

1 Lay the rope out on the ground.

2 Tie the white handkerchief in the middle of the rope.

3 About 3 feet (1 m) on either side of the handkerchief, mark two lines on the ground intersecting the rope.

4 Each team lines up along the rope, facing each other, and takes hold.

5 Take up the tension and when the referee says "Go," both teams pull as hard as they can.

6 If the handkerchief crosses the line nearest your team, you've won.

SKILL LEVEL ◉

TIME NEEDED 15 minutes –½ hour

YOU WILL NEED

A long rope

A white handkerchief or scarf

2 teams of roughly equal sizes and numbers

BALANCING TUG-OF-WAR

If you have limited numbers and different ages/sizes of player, the following variation can ensure that the biggest doesn't always win.

1 Place the stools about 6–12 feet (2–4 m) apart.

2 Lay the rope between the stools, leaving any surplus coiled up at both ends.

3 A player stands on each stool and holds the rope. On starter's orders, you can pull or relax the rope, trying to get the other player to lose balance and step off. Brute strength is not always the answer in this variation. If you tug too hard and your opponent loosens his or her grip, the sudden slack may cause you to fall off.

SKILL LEVEL ◉

TIME NEEDED 15 minutes –½ hour

YOU WILL NEED

2 sturdy crates or stools

A long rope

WARNING

Best played on soft ground in case someone takes a tumble from the stool.

FRENCH BOWLS

The aim of this game is to throw metal balls as close as possible to a small wooden ball called a jack or *cochonnet* (piglet). Known as *pétanque* in its native France, this game is popular all over the world but never more so than in its homeland where around 17 million French families play the game, mostly during their summer vacations. So, *mes amis*, let's play.

SKILL LEVEL	◉
TIME NEEDED	½ hour–1 hour

1 Mark out a starting line on the ground. The players must stand behind this line when throwing their balls.

2 One of the players throws the jack out at a distance of between 20–30 feet (6–10 m) from the starting point.

3 A teammate then plays the first boule, throwing it so that it ends up as close to the jack as possible.

4 Then the opposing team must throw, trying to get closer to the jack. They keep playing until they succeed. When they do, it is back to the first team to do better, and so forth.

5 When one of the teams runs out of boules, the other team plays their remaining boules.

6 When all boules have been played, that is the end of a "round," and the winning team scores a point for each boule that is nearer to the jack than the opposing team's nearest boule.

7 The team that wins a round starts the next one, starting from where the jack ended up in the previous round.

8 The game continues until one of the teams has accumulated 13 points.

YOU WILL NEED

A set of boules (metal balls)

A jack (small wooden ball)

Large open space

Teams of players

DID YOU KNOW?

Pétanque comes from the term *pieds tanqués*, which means "stuck feet," because when playing, your feet should remain fixed together—no stepping.

DODGEBALL

This fast and furious game is so versatile—it can be played indoors or out, you can have as many people in the team as you like and, best of all, you get to throw balls at other people! The rules of dodgeball vary from place to place and school to school, but if you get the hang of these basics, you'll be able to join in and adapt wherever you're invited to play.

SKILL LEVEL ◉ ◉

TIME NEEDED   10 minutes–1 hour

1 There is a strip about 2 feet (0.5 m) wide across the center of the court called the Dead Zone. You'll need to mark this out if you're creating your own dodgeball court to play on. Three balls are placed in the dead zone at the beginning of the game.

2 The two teams (ideally you should have about six people on each team) stand on opposite sides of the Dead Zone.

3 The referee starts the game, which lasts two minutes. Three players from each team run to get the balls. The balls must then be passed to the back line of the court before play starts.

4 The aim is to throw the balls at your opponents (but not at the head), and if they're hit, they are out.

5 If at any time during the game you catch a throw from an opposing player, that person is out and one of your team players comes back in.

6 You win a game when all the opposing team is out, or if you have more players left on court at the end of the two minutes.

YOU WILL NEED

2 teams of 6 players

A space about the size of a badminton or tennis court

3 foam balls

A referee

TOP TIP

Stay inside the court and out of the Dead Zone—if you step over the boundaries, on to the opposing side or into the Dead Zone, you're out. Also watch out for opponents trying to knock the ball from your hands—if they succeed, you're also out.

TABLE TENNIS

Table tennis—also known as ping pong—is a fast and skillful game that demands good reactions. It is the third most popular sport in the world with more than 300 million players worldwide. What's more, it's one of the few games where boys and girls can play on an equal footing because a player doesn't require brute strength to win—technique is more important. If you want to be able to hold your own at ping pong, you need to have a good serve and a killer smash. Master these techniques and you'll have cracked it!

SKILL LEVEL	● ●
TIME NEEDED	½ hour

1 Stand behind the end of the table, holding the ball in the palm of one hand and the paddle in the other.

2 Toss the ball upward about 6–12 inches (15–30 cm) and hit it at the top of its arc. It needs to bounce once on your half of the table (in front of the net) and then once on your opponent's half. In singles games, the ball can land anywhere on your opponent's side of the net, whereas in

doubles games, it must be served diagonally from the right-hand side of your court into the left-hand side of your opponents' court, just as in lawn tennis.

YOU WILL NEED

A table tennis table

2 table tennis paddles

A few table tennis balls

An opponent

DID YOU KNOW?

Did you know? World-class table tennis players can smash the ball at speeds of 70 mph (112.5 km/h)!

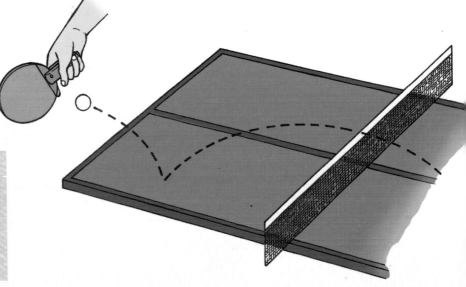

3 If your service is "good," then your opponent must return the ball before it bounces on his or her side of the table a second time. Having service is an advantage because it's hard to return a serve, particularly because you can vary where you place the ball and the speed at which you hit it.

4 Conversely, if your serve hits the net or does not land on your opponent's side, then he or she wins the point. If it hits the net but still goes over to bounce on the other side, that's called a "let," and you take the serve again.

5 Once you've mastered the basic serve, you can confuse your opponent by varying your style between slow serves with lots of spin and faster serves.

THE SMASH

1 Your objective with a smash is to hit the ball so fast that your opponent simply can't return it. You have to wait during a rally for the perfect time to execute a smash shot—usually when your opponent has returned the ball and it bounces high and close to you.

2 Then seize your chance—take a big back-swing, lifting your bat high to account for the higher bounce of the ball. Hit the ball with as much speed as possible onto the other side of the table.

3 Don't rest on your laurels just yet—if your opponent does manage to return your smash, you've got to be on your toes and ready to smash the ball back again until you finally produce the winning shot.

4 This is your trump card when playing table tennis. A good smash moves your opponent out of position and can force her off balance. Her return shot then has to be defensive and you can reply with more smash shots until you win the point.

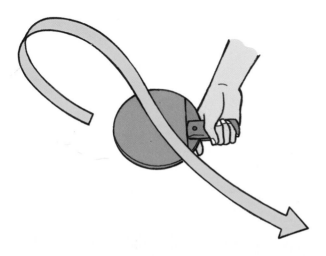

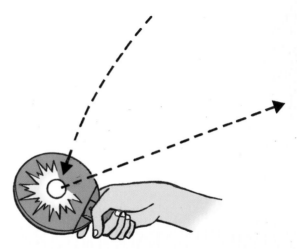

SOFTBALL

If you know how to play baseball, then you'll probably pick up softball really quickly because it too involves hitting a ball with a bat and trying to make it around all the bases. So get your swinging arm at the ready.

SKILL LEVEL ●

TIME NEEDED 1–2 hours

1 Mark out a diamond with 60 feet (18 m) between bases and 40 feet (12 m) from pitcher's mound to home plate.

2 Each team takes turns at batting and then defense.

3 The aim of the team that is batting is to score as many runs as possible by getting runners around all the bases and back to the home plate.

4 A batter is out if the ball is caught in the air; if the ball is caught and thrown at any base before a runner gets there; a runner is tagged by the ball (touched by the ball or the glove of an opposition player) while running between bases; or if three strikes are called by the umpire.

5 A strike is if the ball is pitched outside the strike zone (between batter's armpit and knee), if you swing and miss the ball, or if the pitched ball hits the batter.

6 When three of your batters have been ruled out, then your team is out and the other team comes in to bat.

7 When fielding, the pitcher throws the ball underhand and can only take one step forward to throw.

8 The team with the most points after seven innings, is the winner. If the score is tied, extra innings are played.

YOU WILL NEED

A softball diamond or large playing area and cones

A baseball bat

A softball (slightly bigger—12 inch (30 cm) circumference—and a little softer than a baseball)

Players (officially you need 9 players per team but any even number will do)

DID YOU KNOW?

Softball was originally invented in 1887, as a winter version of the sport of baseball. It was called indoor softball until the 1920s when the name changed to softball and became an organized sport.

WATER VOLLEYBALL

Pools aren't just for swimming—if you have access to a swimming pool, there are plenty of games you can play in the water with a group of people. It is just like ordinary volleyball, but it's played in a pool. This makes it a whole lot harder but also a whole lot cooler so it's ideal for hot summer days! Plus, you don't have the drawback of falling on hard ground when you lunge for the ball.

SKILL LEVEL	◉ ◉
TIME NEEDED	½–1 hour

1 First, set up the net. Stretch it across the center of the swimming pool.

2 Divide your players into two teams of equal numbers. Each team gets into the water, one on either side of the net.

3 The rules are the same as for regular volleyball. So, one team serves and the other team is allowed three hits before the ball must go over the net. If the ball touches the water before going over, it is returned to the other team.

4 If the serving team prevents the opposing team from returning the ball, they score a point.

5 The ball must stay within the pool boundaries or your team is out of the game.

6 The first team to score 15 points wins.

YOU WILL NEED

A swimming pool

A water volleyball net or volleyball net

A volleyball

6 or more players

TOP TIP

You can also try Float Water Volleyball. In this game, the teams sit on inner tubes, which adds a fun twist to the game because you have to paddle with a fury to reach the ball, and no team has the disadvantage of the deep end.

CROQUET

Think of croquet and you'll probably picture a group of ladies in white dresses and parasols playing croquet on the lawn on a hot summer's day in the early 1900s. Actually, the game is still popular today, although, admittedly, it tends to be played with a bit more gusto.

SKILL LEVEL ● ●

TIME NEEDED ½ hour

1 First you need to set up the croquet hoops and agree to the order and direction you are going to play each hoop. You must hit the ball through each hoop in the agreed direction, or it doesn't count.

2 One team plays the blue and black balls and is known as the "cool" team, and the other team plays the red and yellow balls of the set and is known as the "hot" team.

3 The team that goes first plays the blue and black balls. They take turns following the colors on the stake; e.g., blue first, yellow last.

4 Place your ball 3 feet (1 m) south of the first hoop and try to hit it through. You earn another turn if you succeed. If not, your turn is over.

5 If your ball goes through and comes to rest touching another player's ball, you get two bonus strokes (this is known as a "croquet"). You cannot croquet the other team's balls more than once each turn, unless your ball passes through a hoop, but then you still must not croquet the same ball twice in succession.

6 Your ball must pass through the hoops in the agreed order around your course.

7 Once your ball has passed through all of hoops twice (in the right order!), you have to aim for the post. (If you hit the post at any point during the game, you must return your ball to the start.)

8 Take your ball out of play when it hits the final stake.

9 The first team to hit the final stake with both balls is the winner.

YOU WILL NEED

A croquet set (comprising 9 hoops, 2 posts or stakes, 4 mallets, and 4 balls)

A lawn

Two teams

DID YOU KNOW?

A surreal version of croquet featured in Lewis Carroll's *Alice in Wonderland*. Flamingos were used in place of croquet mallets, hedgehogs instead of balls, and soldiers bent over to form the hoops.

EGG AND SPOON RACE

This time-honored playground game requires just the right mix of balancing skills and patience combined with speed and agility. Can you keep the egg on the spoon in the final dash to the line?

SKILL LEVEL	◉ ◉
TIME NEEDED	1 hour

YOU WILL NEED

Dessert spoons

Hard-boiled eggs

2 or more players

Rope

1 Use the rope to lay out a start line and a goal line. Players line up at the start line, balancing the egg on their spoon (remember: you are not allowed to steady the egg with your thumb).

2 When the whistle blows, the first person to get up to the goal line and back without dropping their egg is the winner. (If you drop it, don't worry, you just have to pick it up and carry on!)

3 Whoever makes it back to the start line first is the winner!

SACK RACE

If you can complete the whole course without falling down, you're a better sack racer than most! But then, falling down is half the fun of this crazy game.

SKILL LEVEL	◉
TIME NEEDED	1 hour

YOU WILL NEED

Some old pillowcases or burlap sacks

Ropes

1 Using the rope, lay out a start line and a finish line.

2 Each contestant climbs into a sack, holding the edges of the sack up around the waist.

3 On the starter's whistle, they must hop from the start line to the finish line.

4 If you fall down (and you probably will) just get up and carry on once you've managed to stop laughing!

WARNING

Because it is so easy to trip and fall during the sack race, make sure you set your course on grass or some other soft surface.

THREE-LEGGED RACE

A firm favorite of the parish picnic, the three-legged race is also popular with college students as an annual fundraising event. Basically, you're never too old to join in with this laugh-a-minute game—especially when you trip and fall, as you inevitably will!

SKILL LEVEL ◉

TIME NEEDED 1 hour

1 Use the two ropes to mark a starting line and a finish line. Divide players into pairs. Each player stands next to his partner and puts his arm around his partner's waist.

2 The partners' inside legs should be touching. Tie the partners' inside legs together so each pair has three legs rather than four.

3 The players line up at the starting line. On the signal, players walk or run as fast as they can to the finish line.

4 Sound easy? You'll be surprised how difficult it can be to make two legs work as one! The winners are the pair that crosses the finish line first.

YOU WILL NEED

Scarves or strips of fabric long enough for tying legs together (one for each pair of contestants)

2 ropes

TOP TIP

You will hop and run more efficiently if you push your toes into the bottom corners of the sack. To avoid any arguments, decide before the event starts whether or not running is allowed or if all contestants must hop in their sacks.

LEAPFROG

Believe it or not, there is evidence that the Ancient Egyptians played Leap Frog, which they called Knuzza Iawizza. Seems that a good playground game will always stand the test of time. So why not put a spring in your step and give it a try.

SKILL LEVEL	◉
TIME NEEDED	5 minutes

1 Each player stands side by side in a line. Space out, and when in position, the players should kneel down and rest their heads on the ground, covered by their hands.

2 Stand at the back of the line, and place your hands on the back of the person at the back of the line. Press down on the person's back and leap over them, spreading your legs apart like a frog.

3 Continue hopping over players until you reach the front of the line, where you then kneel down and cover your head,

ready for the next person at the back of the line to leapfrog.

4 The game continues for as long as you like or until you run out of space. Then you can turn around and come back again!

YOU WILL NEED

At least 2 people, but the more the merrier

TOP TIP

As you get more confident, the "obstacles" can get higher. Players can bend over rather than kneeling down, making sure to brace themselves by putting their hands on their thighs and tucking their heads right in for safety.

FRISBEE

Whether you're on the beach, at a picnic, or in your own backyard, nothing beats the versatility of the Frisbee. You can play catch with friends, fetch with the dog, or teach yourself new tricks. There are hours of wrist-flicking entertainment to be had from this simple-looking object. If the standard game of throwing the Frisbee to each other starts to get a bit repetitive, there are plenty of variations you can try.

SKILL LEVEL	◉ ◉
TIME NEEDED	5 minutes

FRISBEE BOULES

Throw a tennis ball on the lawn, then take turns trying to land a Frisbee as close to it as possible. The player who gets the Frisbee nearest to the ball wins.

TRICK FRISBEE

Impress your friends by spinning a Frisbee on your finger. Simply spray a light coating of vegetable oil or silicone spray on the underside of the Frisbee. When it glides down toward you, raise your hand with your forefinger extended and just center it under the Frisbee as it lands. It will continue to spin and amaze all onlookers.

FANCY CATCHES

Another way to look good is to do a flashy catch. A good one for novices is the flamingo. When a slow, flat throw about knee high comes your way, raise one leg high behind you and with the opposite hand behind your standing leg, catch the disk. You'll look so cool. Other tricks known to impress are catching it behind your back or while leaping in the air.

YOU WILL NEED

A Frisbee

At least 2 people, but more can join in

DID YOU KNOW?

The record for the longest Frisbee toss by an under 15-year-old girl is held by American Mary Uhlarik who threw it 410.4 ft (125.1 m) on November 4, 1994, at Anaheim, California.

JUMPING ROPE

Jumping rope, or skipping as it's also called, is a great way to get in shape, and it's fun. It's one of the few games you can play on your own or with your friends and, if you have a long rope, you can even skip in groups.

SKILL LEVEL ◉

TIME NEEDED   5 minutes

BASIC JUMP

1 Hold the handles of the rope in each hand with the rope behind you. Swing the rope over your head.

2 Keeping both feet together, as the rope comes down in front of you toward the ground, jump over it.

3 Repeat this 10 times or until you get tangled up, whichever comes first.

4 Once you've mastered this, you've got the basics of skipping. Congratulations! Now it's time to move on.

YOU WILL NEED

A jump rope or skipping rope

Bags of energy!

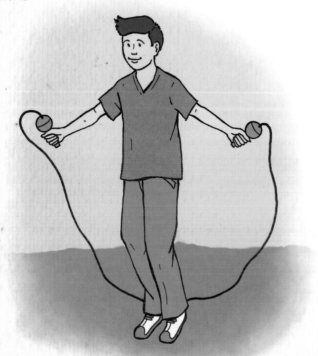

DOUBLE TURN

This one is quite an advanced trick and, to succeed, you'll need to jump high and turn the rope as fast as you can. Good luck!

1 Start with a normal, single bounce from the basic jump.

2 Then, jump high into the air and turn the rope fast so that it passes beneath your feet twice before you land.

FRONT STRADDLE

1 Turn the rope and jump with one foot in front and the other behind.

2 As the rope comes around again, jump again but switch the position of your legs.

FRONT CROSS

This one will really impress your friends.

1 Do a normal jump with the first turn of the rope.

2 As the rope comes around for the next turn, cross your arms in front of you and jump through the loop it makes.

3 Try switching between front cross jumps and normal jumps if you want to look like a true pro.

CHINESE JUMP ROPE

Success at Chinese jump rope relies on skill and agility rather than strength. Below is an example of a jump pattern, but there are many routines in circulation that you can play for variation, or you can make up your own. Many of these routines are performed while chanting a rhyme. Why not ask your mom if she can remember any from her playground days?

SKILL LEVEL ●

TIME NEEDED 15 minutes

1 Get your two friends to stand opposite each other with the loop around their ankles, holding it apart with their feet at hip width.

2 You will be the jumper first. Start by standing with your feet straddling the left-hand side of the elastic. Then jump so that your feet land straddling the right-hand length of elastic.

3 Next, jump so both feet land inside the elastic loop and then jump and land with both feet outside the elastic loop.

4 Repeat step 2 and then finish by jumping and landing with both feet together to the side of the elastic.

5 If completed successfully, the height of the elastic is raised to the knees and the jump pattern repeated, then the elastic is raised to the thighs, waist, and so on.

6 If you fail at a jump at any level, you replace one of the players holding the elastic and then it's their turn.

7 Once you've mastered the basics, the game can be made more difficult: skinny (using only one foot to hold the elastic); wide (legs as far apart as possible); blind (jumper's eyes closed); cross-over (the elastic closest to the jumper is crossed over the far elastic and the routine completed in the resulting triangle of elastic).

8 The game can also be played in teams, where, if the first jumper makes a mistake, the second jumper must then complete the routine twice.

YOU WILL NEED

A piece of sewing elastic sewn in a loop

3 or more people to play

TOP TIP

If you don't have any sewing elastic, you can link large elastic bands together to form a long loop.

JACKS

This is a game of skill that is not only fun to play, but also very useful to help you improve your hand-eye coordination. You'll find that good coordination skills can help in all manner of ways in modern life, not least in sports and video games.

SKILL LEVEL ●

TIME NEEDED 15 minutes

1 To start, throw the five jacks on the ground and then pick up the ball.

2 Now, throw the ball up in the air, and with the same hand, pick up one jack and then catch the ball before it hits the ground.

3 Put the retrieved jack in your other hand. Repeat until all the jacks have been picked up.

4 Now throw the jacks back on the floor and start again, but this time, two jacks must be picked up each time except for the final throw when, obviously, only one jack is picked up.

5 If you succeed at this round, you play again but picking up three jacks and then again with four jacks, and finally the ball is thrown up and all five jacks are picked up at once before the ball is caught.

6 If you miss the ball or don't manage to pick up the right number of jacks, your turn is over and the next player has a try. If you're playing on your own, you go back to the beginning of that round.

YOU WILL NEED

5 jacks (6-pronged, metal, and tipped with a ball on the end of each prong)

A small bouncy ball

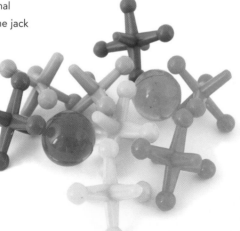

TOP TIP

In some countries, the ball is allowed to bounce once before it must be caught. This makes the game a little easier. On the other hand, if you're a real whiz at Jacks, try putting in a clap of the hands before the pickup.

CRAFTS AND ACTIVITIES

For those days when you're feeling creative, there
are plenty of activities and crafts, for outdoors or
indoors. From making sundials and face painting to
folding the perfect paper airplanes and weaving
your own basket, you'll find all sorts of creative
projects to keep yourself, and your friends,
entertained all day long.

MAKE A BASKET

Basket weaving is one of the oldest known crafts, even pre-dating pottery making, and the skill has been handed down through the generations. If you imagine that practically any container or packaging that is now made from plastic, cardboard, or plywood would once have been made of basketry, it gives you an idea of the importance of basket makers throughout history. Although it's probably a bit too ambitious to attempt to make a traditional willow basket from scratch, you can start with a paper basket to get the hang of the principles.

SKILL LEVEL	◉ ◉
TIME NEEDED	½ hour

1 Cut each sheet of paper into long strips about a ½ inch (12 mm) wide. Lay out 12 strips of the same color (red, for example) next to each other in vertical lines, then count out 12 strips of the other color (we'll say green for this example).

2 Take a green strip and, starting about a third of the way down, horizontally weave it over the first vertical red strip on the right and under the next, repeating this over and under movement until you reach the other side. Pull the strip through so that you have roughly equal ends protruding on each side of the vertical strips.

3 Take the next green strip and weave it horizontally through the red vertical strips starting just below your first green strip.

4 Continue weaving the strips until all 24 have been used.

YOU WILL NEED

2 large sheets of construction paper in different colors (say green and red)

A stapler or craft glue

5 Try to keep the weaving as neat and even as possible so that you end up with a reasonably tight checkerboard effect.

6 You should now have a woven base with green strips extending on two opposite sides and red strips extending on the other two opposite sides.

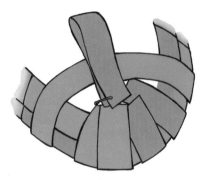

7 Gather up all of the strips on one side. Bend them upward and collect them into the middle to form a fan shape that is broader at the base, so that all the ends of the strips come together. Staple or glue the ends where they meet.

8 Repeat this step with the strips on the other three sides.

9 Take two more red strips and two more green strips. Put them into pairs (it's up to you whether you mix your colors or keep like with like). Attach one end of one pair of strips to a corner (top of the fan) and cross it over the center of the basket and attach to the opposite corner.

10 Take the last remaining pair of strips and repeat step 9 using the other two corners of the basket.

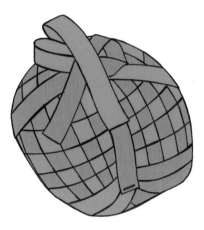

11 You can leave your handle plain or you might like to make a paper bow to attach to it as a decoration. These attractive baskets look fabulous filled with brightly wrapped candies.

DID YOU KNOW?

Traces of baskets have been found in the Egyptian pyramids, and woven basket liners have left their impressions inside the fragments of ancient pottery. Baskets were needed as containers for everything – food, clothing, seeds, storage, and transport.

GARDENING

Contrary to popular myth, you do not have to be a senior citizen to enjoy gardening. In fact, you'd be amazed how many celebrities cite gardening as a way of relaxing. Perhaps you haven't caught the gardening bug yet, but you will.

SKILL LEVEL	◉ ◉
TIME NEEDED	20 minutes to plant, 4–6 weeks to grow

GROWING HERBS

Herbs have been used for thousands of years. They have been added to dishes, used as perfumes, remedies, and even as currency. These days you're most likely to use them in the kitchen to add flavor to your food, and there are all sorts of different herbs available. Growing your own herbs means you'll always have an abundance of different ones to try. If cooking isn't your thing, you can just enjoy all the different scents they provide.

YOU WILL NEED

Containers of various sizes

Your choice of herb plants in pots (available from garden centers)

Good multipurpose potting mix

A trowel

1 Make sure all of your chosen containers have good drainage. If you're using plastic pots, you can carefully poke a hole in the bottom with an awl or a screwdriver.

2 Fill the containers three-quarters full with potting mix.

3 When choosing your herbs, think about which ones might be used more regularly for cooking in your household. Do you like mint and basil, or maybe rosemary and thyme?

4 Don't forget to check the labels to see how big the plants can grow. Did you know angelica can grow to more than 6 feet (1.8 m) tall, for example? Make sure your garden won't get so big it takes over the whole kitchen!

5 Allocate herbs to each pot according to how big the plants grow, and how likely you are to use them in your cooking.

6 Tip the seedlings out of their little pots and plant them in your containers. Surround them with more potting mix, press them down a little to make sure they're secure (but not so much that the soil is packed together), and give them a little water.

7 Then arrange your pots attractively on a windowsill where they will get plenty of sunlight, and watch them grow!

8 If you're pressed for space, you can grow herbs in strawberry pots with something large like lavender and chives in the main part and other herbs in the side holes. Or you can even plant them in hanging baskets.

9 You must make sure your containers are well-watered because the herbs tend to dry out more quickly than if they were planted in the backyard.

GROWING A SUNFLOWER

Growing plenty of colorful flowers can instantly transform your backyard into your own little summer retreat, and few flowers are as summery as a sunflower. It's also a great place to start for those of you who are looking for a challenge because sunflowers can be a bit tricky to grow.

SKILL LEVEL	●
TIME NEEDED	15 minutes to plant, 2–3 months to grow

1 In spring, after the danger of frost has passed, find a clear flowerbed in a nice, sunny spot and loosen the soil with a trowel. Then plant your seeds 4–6 inches (10–15 cm) apart and cover them with a ½ in (12 mm) of soil.

2 Water them just enough to keep the soil moist—don't overwater them or they won't grow. Keep watering them as the seeds sprout and your miniature sunflower plants start to develop. Check the soil once or twice a week to make sure that it's not bone-dry. Your plants should soon start to shoot up into tall, straight stems with large, flat leaves.

3 Expect the flowers to develop in the late summer and early fall. As the flowers start to fade, cut the dead heads off to encourage new flowers to grow in their place.

4 If your variety is an annual (i.e., has a lifespan of just one year), pull the plants out and discard them in the fall, once they have been exposed to frost. If you chose a perennial variety (i.e., one that blooms each year), then just cut them down and wait until next year for them to flower again.

5 You can give your sunflower a head start during a cold spring by planting the seed in a little pot on your windowsill and letting it grow into a seedling indoors. Then you can plant the seedling rather than seeds in your garden. Don't forget to water your little pot regularly, or your seedlings won't get started!

YOU WILL NEED

A garden trowel

Sunflower seeds (available from garden centers and supermarkets)

A watering can

A garden spade

CREATE A TERRARIUM

Terrariums are enclosed glass containers filled with soil and plants. Because they're sealed up, water inside condenses on the sides and top of the glass and runs back down into the soil—automatic rain! You hardly ever have to water a terrarium, but you do get to watch the plants grow from seeds to grown-ups in a couple of weeks.

SKILL LEVEL ◉

TIME NEEDED 1 hour

1 Line the bottom of the jar with peat moss and scatter a layer of gravel over the top.

2 On top of the gravel, put down a layer of potting mix for your plants to grow in. The moss-gravel-soil layers should be at least 3 inches (7.5 cm) thick.

3 Plant a few seedlings or plants in the jar—you don't want it to be too crowded. Use long tweezers or tongs to make small holes and to lower plants into the jar. Cover their roots and tamp soil loosely around them. If you're sowing seeds, spread soil lightly over the top.

4 Water the plants lightly— about ½ cup (125 ml) of water should be enough. If your plants get too wet, the soil will turn to marsh and nothing will grow except mold.

5 Use a screwdriver or other sharp device to poke three or four small holes in the jar lid. Terrariums need ventilation so mold doesn't grow inside. Screw the lid onto the jar.

6 Place the terrarium in a well-lit place near a window, but not in direct sunlight because that can burn the plants inside.

7 Watch your plants grow! If you want to add more life, find a few insects in your backyard that eat plants and settle them in. Be careful not to have too many, though, or they'll eat faster than your plants can grow.

8 Every few months, scrape off the top layer of potting soil and replace it with fresh stuff, to keep your plants nourished.

YOU WILL NEED

A large glass jar with a wide opening and a metal lid

Clumps or sheets of peat moss

Long tweezers or tongs that can fit inside the jar opening

Gravel

Potting mix

Small plants that like humid environments

A funnel

A screwdriver

BUILDING A SUNDIAL

Sundials are the world's oldest clocks—they work on the simple principle that the sun is always in the same direction at noon: directly south in the northern hemisphere, and directly north in the southern hemisphere. By making your own sundial, you can tell time using the sun and the shadows it creates.

SKILL LEVEL	☀
TIME NEEDED	6 hours

1 Turn the shoebox on its end. Draw a circle in the middle of one end.

2 Using a screwdriver, poke a hole in the middle of the circle. Then poke a hole in the bottom of the shoebox below the first hole, but a little further back.

3 Push your stick through the first hole and angle it back toward the end of the shoebox. Push the tip of the stick through the second hole you made and tape it in place. Your stick should now poke up at an angle out of the circle on the top of the box.

4 Take your sundial outside and place it on a flat surface.

5 Use a compass to find north, and point the stick in that direction if you're in the northern hemisphere, or south if you're in the southern hemisphere. The stick should throw a good, clear shadow across the circle you drew.

6 At exactly 9 A.M, draw a line marking the position of the shadow of the stick on the circle you drew in step 1. Mark it with a straight line and label it 9 A.M.

7 Each hour after that, revisit your sundial and mark the new location of the shadow up until 3 P.M. Your sundial is now ready to tell the time. If you want your sundial to work earlier or later during the day, you have to keep on marking the shadow on the hour.

8 Any time you want to use the sundial, take it outside and use your compass to point the stick in the right direction, as you did in step 5. Then see where the shadow falls across the lines you drew.

YOU WILL NEED

A shoebox

A screwdriver

A straight stick—bamboo works well

Masking tape

A black marker

A compass

A full sunny day

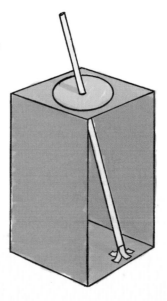

MAKING PANPIPES

Panpipes have been in use for thousands of years in civilizations all across the world. In Ancient Greece, they were made out of reeds and associated with the woodland god Pan (which is where they get their modern name). In the Andes, they are made from bamboo and known as *siku* or *zampoña*.

SKILL LEVEL ●

TIME NEEDED   20 minutes – ½ hour

1 You're going to cut your plastic piping into five panpipes, so measure out the following pieces: 12 ½ inches (31 cm), 11 inches (28 cm), 10 inches (25 cm), 8 ½ inches (21 cm), and 7 inches (18 cm). Use the saw to cut the lengths out as smoothly as possible.

2 Seal the bottom of each pipe with a piece of modeling clay. Make sure no air can get out through the bottom.

3 Unroll a piece of adhesive tape 5 inches (12.5 cm) long and lay it, sticky-side up, on the table. Arrange the pipes in order of size in the middle of the tape, making sure to keep the top ends (the ends without the clay) at the same level.

4 Wrap the rest of the tape around the front of your set of pipes and you're ready to play. Blow gently across the top of a pipe. Don't blow too hard, and don't blow down into the pipe. If you can't get a sound out, make sure the bottom of the pipe is sealed. Now have a try playing a tune.

YOU WILL NEED

A piece of plastic pipe, 49 in (123 cm) long and a ½ in (1.2 cm) in diameter

A small saw

Modeling clay

A measuring tape

Adhesive tape

DID YOU KNOW?

Panpipes get their name from Greek mythology. The god Pan pursued a water nymph named Syrinx. She was transformed into reeds in order to escape him. When the air blew through the reeds, it produced a plaintive melody. Pan cut the reeds and joined them side by side to create his panpipe.

SOAP-POWERED BOATS

Did you know that soap can power a paper boat? That's because when soap is mixed with water it disrupts one of water's properties, known as surface tension. Surface tension is what's responsible when you place a leaf or small piece of paper on top of water and it floats instead of sinking. That's because water is made up of hydrogen and oxygen atoms, which form molecules that stick very close together. The forces holding the molecules together essentially create a "skin" at the water's surface, which prevents small objects from breaking through. That's surface tension. The ingredients in soap can disrupt the forces that hold the water molecules together, and so dissolve the surface tension. This is how we can use soap to power a paper boat, by using soap to disrupt the surface tension on just one side of the model.

SKILL LEVEL ◉

TIME NEEDED   20 minutes –½ hour

1 On the card, draw out a flat boat with a pointed tip and round sides. It shouldn't be too large. Include a notch 1 inch (2.5 cm) across and ½ inch (1.2 cm) deep in the back of the boat.

2 Angle the sides of the notch outward. This is where we're going to pour the liquid soap later.

3 Cut out the boat along the lines you've drawn.

4 Fill a baking dish with water. Place the flat boat on top of the water at one end of the baking dish. The surface tension should hold it floating on top of the water.

5 Put a few drops of liquid soap in the notch at the back of the boat. The soap breaks down the surface tension of the water at the back of the boat, but not at the front or around the sides. Because there is an imbalance in the forces acting on the boat, it should be pushed gently forward.

6 You must clean out the baking dish after each try or the boat won't move the next time.

YOU WILL NEED

A sheet of thin cardboard paper, or an index card

A pencil

A pair of scissors

A rectangular glass baking dish

Liquid soap

MAKING A SODA GEYSER

One of the great things about science is that it's always advancing. This can get a bit messy, so make sure you're wearing old clothes when you try it. This experiment was first discovered by putting mint-flavored candies into soda, but table salt works just as well, if not better. All you need is a wide open space, a few groceries, and a willingness to get wet.

SKILL LEVEL ◉

TIME NEEDED   20 minutes –½ hour

1 Take all your ingredients outside and away from anything that you don't want to cover in diet soda. This is a very messy experiment.

2 Roll the piece of paper loosely into a tube and pour a good handful of salt into it. Hold one end of the tube to keep the salt in.

3 Take the cap off of the bottle. From arm's length, hold the tube over the bottle and funnel all the salt into the soda.

4 Try and run away before the geyser covers you in soda.

Bubbles in soda are made by dissolving carbon dioxide gas in water used to make the drink. When salt or candies enter the soda, they cause all the carbon dioxide to come out of solution very quickly, shooting out of the bottle in a foamy jet.

YOU WILL NEED

A bottle of diet soda

Table salt

A sheet of paper

A big outdoor space

MAKING A BUBBLE BOMB

Experimenting with household materials and substances wouldn't be any fun if your mixtures didn't sometimes produce a reaction. Of course, some scientists have blown up their labs by combining the wrong things, but we won't go that far. Here's a way we can cause some harmless commotion.

SKILL LEVEL ◉

TIME NEEDED 20 minutes

1 Pick a good outdoor spot to do the experiment.

2 Make sure your bag has no holes in it—fill it up with water first as a test.

3 Using a pair of scissors, cut a paper towel into four equal-sized squares.

4 Put 1½ tablespoons (20 ml) of baking soda in the middle of one square and fold all four sides of the paper towel over the baking soda. This is going to go into the vinegar—the paper stops the baking soda from getting out right away, so you've got time to get clear. Pouring baking soda directly into the vinegar won't give you enough time to close the bag.

5 Fill the bag with ½ cup (125 ml) vinegar and 1 cup (250 ml) warm water.

6 Drop your baking soda/paper towel package into the solution and quickly zip the bag closed.

7 Place the bag down carefully and quickly stand back.

8 The vinegar and the baking soda produce a chemical reaction that forms bubbles of carbon dioxide. As the gas in the bubbles expands, it creates pressure that will eventually pop the bag!

YOU WILL NEED

Vinegar

Baking (bicarbonate) soda

Warm water

A ziplock bag

A pair of scissors

Paper towel

A measuring cup

Measuring spoons

This is a classic example of a chemical reaction. Chemical reactions take place when two chemicals combine to create new substances. Vinegar is a weak acid (known as "acetic acid"), and baking soda contains a chemical called sodium bicarbonate. Acids react with bicarbonates to create carbon dioxide gas, water, and a salt. The part we're interested in is the carbon dioxide gas. Because we've sealed the bag shut, the gas creates pressure as it's given off. When the pressure is high enough, the bag can't contain it any longer and bursts.

WARNING

The liquid in the bag will sting if it gets into your eyes. Make sure you're standing far from the bag when it pops.

MEASURING AIR PRESSURE

Low pressure means wind and rain, and high pressure means warm days in summer, and cold days in winter. Meteorologists use an instrument called a barometer to measure air pressure. If you want to know what weather the day holds in store for you, and whether its going to ruin your picnic plans, you can construct a simple one by yourself very easily.

SKILL LEVEL ●
TIME NEEDED   20 minutes

1 Cut a circle out of the balloon and stretch it over the top of the jar to create a tight seal, like a drum. Carefully stick one end of the straw to the middle of the balloon, so the rest of the straw pokes out over the side of the jar.

2 Glue one edge of the cardboard to the side of the jar so that the straw sticks out across it. Mark the exact position of the straw on the cardboard. Check the straw every day and mark its new position on the cardboard.

YOU WILL NEED

A glass jar

A balloon

A drinking straw

Glue

A piece of thin cardboard or card stock

A fine-tipped pen or sharp pencil

When you stretch the balloon over the jar, you seal air inside at whatever the air pressure is at that moment. If the pressure outside the jar drops, the membrane will swell, because the pressure inside will be higher by comparison. This will push the tip of the straw down. If the air pressure rises, the pressure inside the jar will be relatively low, and the membrane will sag inward, pushing the tip of the straw up.

TOP TIP

The straw will probably only move a very small amount. Make sure your marks are very accurate so you can notice the differences.

MEASURING WIND SPEED

Wind is always around us, whether it's a gentle breeze that just rustles the leaves on a summer's day or a hurricane that threatens to tear the roof off our houses. Wind is always gusting around the globe. But where does it come from? What is wind?

SKILL LEVEL   ◉

TIME NEEDED   20 minutes

Wind is the movement of air across the surface of the Earth. It happens because of shifts in air pressure (see page 91), which change according to the temperature, and the movement of the Earth spinning on its axis. Wind is what we feel when air shifts from an area of high pressure to an area of low pressure.

Lots of people depend on wind for their work and their experiments. Weather scientists (or meteorologists) check the wind to give weather forecasts; pilots constantly check wind patterns when they're flying; and sailors, even on boats with engines, always have to know when the wind is coming and which way it's going to blow.

There are lots of different ways to check wind speed. Scientists use instruments called "anemometers," which come in a variety of different designs. Simple ones have a propeller blade or a series of cups mounted on a wheel, which spin in the wind. The instrument measures how fast they're spinning

and uses that data to calculate the wind speed.

One easy experiment for measuring wind speed without an anemometer is to use a ping pong ball suspended on the end of a string. Setting this one up shouldn't take more than 10 minutes. Then you have to wait for the leaves to start rustling.

1 Tape one end of the string to the ping pong ball, and tape the other end to the center point of the protractor's straight edge.

2 Find a spot out in the open where the wind won't be blocked by trees or buildings.

3 Hold the protractor upside-down, so the string hangs down across the face. Stand with your back to the wind and let the string and the ping pong ball hang in the wind. The wind will blow the ping pong ball out sideways so that the string will be pulled at an angle across the protractor.

YOU WILL NEED

A ping pong ball

10 in (25 cm) of string

A protractor

Adhesive tape

A notebook and pen

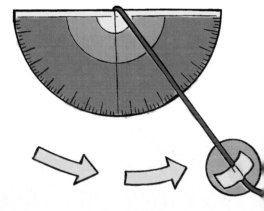

4 Use the wind speed scale below to determine how fast the wind is moving. The stronger the wind, the sharper (or smaller) the angle will be. If there's no wind at all the ball will hang straight down, so the protractor will read a 90-degree angle.

5 Record wind speeds over the course of a day, making sure to also record the time each measurement was taken. You may want to take note of the weather and temperature at the time of your measurements, and see if any patterns or relationships can be found.

6 If you record the direction the wind was blowing from along with the wind speed, by taking a compass with you, you can add that to your list of data. Bad weather often blows in from the same direction—use your data to work out which direction that is around your home.

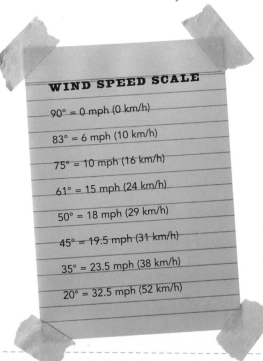

WIND SPEED SCALE

90° = 0 mph (0 km/h)

83° = 6 mph (10 km/h)

75° = 10 mph (16 km/h)

61° = 15 mph (24 km/h)

50° = 18 mph (29 km/h)

45° = 19.5 mph (31 km/h)

35° = 23.5 mph (38 km/h)

20° = 32.5 mph (52 km/h)

MOVING WATER UPHILL

Water will always flow downhill, right? Wrong. In certain situations water can actually flow upward!

SKILL LEVEL	◉
TIME NEEDED	20 minutes

YOU WIL NEED

A tall glass

Water

Food coloring

Clear plastic tubing of various diameters, from pencil-thickness to the thinnest you can find

Trees get water from the ground up to their leaves by a process called capillary action. A capillary is a tiny tube about the width of a hair. When liquid enters into these tiny tubes, it is drawn along their length, as you can see for yourself in this activity.

1 Fill a glass half full with water. Add a few drops of food coloring so you can see the level.

2 Put one end of the largest clear plastic tube in the glass of water and watch as the level of water in the tube rises a little.

3 Now try the thinner tubes. The water should climb higher the thinner the tubes get.

A KALEIDOSCOPE

"Kaleidoscope" comes from the Greek words that mean "beautiful view," and that's just what you get when you look through the end of one of these tubes. But the view isn't of a magical and colorful island in the clouds. You're looking at a collection of shiny bits of paper and beads that are reflected many times by a set of mirrors. All you need to make your own kaleidoscope (and the beautiful view that comes with it) is a few simple materials, and about an hour.

SKILL LEVEL	
TIME NEEDED	½ hour–40 minutes

1 Place each mirror on a sheet of cardboard and trace around it with a pencil.

2 Cut the cardboard along the pencil lines so that you end up with three rectangular pieces the same size as the mirrors.

3 Tape the mirrors to the cardboard. Try not to get too much tape on the front of the mirrors or you'll see it in your view.

cardboard and mirror together. The mirrors should be facing inward, and you should tape them as tightly together as you can so there are no gaps.

4 Create a triangular tube by taping all three pieces of

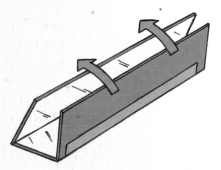

5 Cut out 2 triangular pieces of tracing paper that will fit exactly over the end of the triangular tube. Tape these pieces of tracing paper together on two sides so that you form a triangular envelope.

YOU WILL NEED

Thin cardboard or card stock

Scissors

3 small rectangular mirrors

Clear adhesive tape

Tracing paper

Very small, shiny, and colorful pieces of paper cut into fun shapes

A pencil

DID YOU KNOW?

The kaleidoscope was originally conceived by Ancient Greek mathematicians. But the knowledge was lost over the centuries, until it was reinvented in 1816 by a Scottish scientist called David Brewster. He originally designed it as a science experiment, but it quickly became more popular as a toy.

6 Fill the triangular envelope with small pieces of shiny paper cutouts through the un-taped side. Don't overfill it—you want to allow the shiny pieces of paper to move around freely inside.

7 When the envelope is filled to your liking, tape the third side of it closed to seal in the shiny pieces of paper. Then tape the triangle over one end of the kaleidoscope tube.

8 Next, cut out a triangular piece of cardboard to fit over the opposite end of the tube and tape it in place.

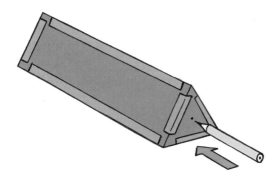

9 Use your pencil and poke an eyehole into the triangular cardboard end. Your kaleidoscope is now ready.

10 To use the kaleidoscope, point it toward the light and look through the eyehole. The light coming into the tube will reflect off the mirrors and create symmetrical patterns around the little bits of paper. To get a new design, shake the kaleidoscope and look again.

PAPER AIRPLANES

All you really need to make a paper plane is a sheet of paper—unless you plan to make an entire air force, which, by the way, might be fun!

SKILL LEVEL	
TIME NEEDED	10 minutes

YOU WILL NEED

A rectangular sheet of paper

1 Fold the paper in half lengthwise to create a crease, then unfold it. Fold it in half widthwise to create another crease.

2 Unfold the paper and lay it flat. Turn it so the short side is toward you, and fold the top of the paper down so it meets the widthwise crease.

3 Fold the corners on that side in so they meet at the lengthwise center crease, then fold the tip of the plane down onto itself to make a blunt nose for the plane.

4 Fold the plane in half along the lengthwise center crease.

5 Next make the wings. Fold one side down then flip the plane over and fold the other side down. Leave about a ½ inch (1 cm) on the body of the plane to hold onto.

6 You can fly your paper plane inside or take it outside if it's a nice day!

BLOWING PERFECT BUBBLES

To blow really big, long-lasting bubbles, you need to add a magic ingredient to your detergent-and-water mix. Then, with a few clever twists of wire, you can make fantastic bubble wands and spend hours of fun outside creating perfect bubbles.

SKILL LEVEL	●
TIME NEEDED	20 minutes

1 Combine the water, dish-washing liquid, and glucose syrup in a large, shallow container, and leave the mixture to rest for a couple of hours.

2 To make your bubble wand: hold the coat hanger by the hook, pull the opposite end down to open out the loop.

3 Using the wire-cutters, cut off the hook and the neck of the hanger, and then straighten out the remaining wire to give you a straight piece of wire.

4 Using needle-nose pliers, twist a small hook at one end of the wire. Make it about as big as the wire is around.

5 Bend that end around, and hook it onto the wire about 9 inches (23 cm) from the opposite end. This should give you a circle at the end of your wand about 7 inches (18 cm) in diameter.

6 Squeeze the hook with pliers around the wire, to hold the circle in place, and straighten the long end of the wire. At the bottom, bunch the last few inches together to form a handle, so you get a good grip when the time comes to start making bubbles.

7 Cut a circle of floral netting or chicken wire about 8 inches (20 cm) in diameter. With pliers, fold the netting's edge tightly around the frame, snipping off any sharp ends. You should now have a long bubble wand with a loop at the end that has wire mesh across it.

8 You're ready to blow some bubbles. Just dip your wand into the mixture, and either wave it through the air or blow through the mesh—blowing gently but steadily is the best way to make them grow.

YOU WILL NEED

10 cups (2.5 l) of water

4 cups (1 l) of dish washing liquid

1 cup (250 ml) of glucose syrup

A plastic-coated wire clothes hanger

Floral netting or plastic-coated chicken wire

Wire cutters

Needle-nose pliers

MAKING A CLAY POT

Pottery is one of the oldest human technologies and art-forms, and we're still making it today. Here's a chance to try your hand at this craft and make your own little clay pot. The type used by professional potters needs to be fired (baked) at very high temperatures, but you can buy hobby clay from craft stores that will either dry by itself or can be baked in a home oven. This project can get messy, so put on an apron or overall to cover your clothes, and make sure you have a hard, flat surface to work on—one that won't stain.

SKILL LEVEL	◉ ◉
TIME NEEDED	1–2 hours

1 Warm the clay by kneading it with your hands. If you keep folding it over on top of itself, you will create air bubbles (which you want to avoid) so after kneading, throw the ball back and forth quite roughly between your hands or throw it onto a hard surface (like a worktop) several times.

2 Once the clay is soft and pliable, roll it into a long "worm" that's about a ½ inch (12 mm) in diameter and about 12–24 inches (30–60 cm) long. Keep the width of the worm as consistent as possible all the way down to avoid bulges in your pot.

3 Take one end of the "worm" and start to coil it into a tight circle. Continue to coil it around itself, making sure the coils are pressed together, until you've

created a circular base for your pot. (You can mold it into a smooth base if you prefer by scraping a straight edge across the surface.) Cut the "worm" where the coil finishes, and secure the end by molding it onto the coil.

4 Now you can start the sides of the pot. Take the end of your clay "worm" and coil it around the outside of the base. Press it down firmly and then, on the inside of your pot (while supporting the outside wall with the other hand so it doesn't bow out), smooth down with your fingertips to seal the gap between the bottom and the coil.

YOU WILL NEED

Air-dried or home-oven fired clay

An apron or old shirt (to protect your clothes)

Poster paints

Decorations, e.g., fake gems, baubles, glitter, etc. (optional)

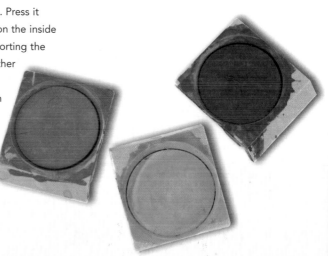

5 As you reach the end of the first coil, allow the worm to overlap and continue building the wall, smoothing down each time.

6 Once you've reached the desired height (or the end of your worm), level out the top row by flattening it down slightly and trimming down the end.

7 Make sure the inside is completely smoothed out—wetting your fingers makes this easier.

8 If you are having trouble removing your pot from the work surface, take a piece of string and wrap it around a couple of fingers on both hands (rather like dental floss) and, pulling the string tight, "saw" the string back and forth, pulling it toward you underneath the pot.

9 If you're using home-oven clay, then follow the instructions that came with it to bake it solid. This clay is best baked on an oven-safe glass surface. For air-dry clay, just leave the pot out overnight until it hardens.

10 Once your clay is fully dry, you can paint the pot. Put on two coats, and glue on any other decorations you fancy.

PRESSING FLOWERS

Whether you use them for making home-made greetings cards or for displays, pressed flowers can be as beautiful as the fresh variety. And what's more, they last forever.

SKILL LEVEL	
TIME NEEDED	20 minutes

YOU WILL NEED

A selection of your favorite flowers or foliage, picked and ready to go

A heavy book such as a telephone directory or dictionary

A sheet of newspaper

1 Arrange the flowers on one half of the sheet of newspaper, being careful to ensure that the leaves and petals do not overlap.

2 Then fold the top half of the newspaper sheet down over the flowers.

3 Open the heaviest book in the middle and place the newspaper on the open page. Close the book and place the other books or heavy objects on top.

4 After about three days, open the book and carefully remove the pressed flowers from the newspaper. They're now ready to use.

PAPIER MÂCHÉ

The Chinese were the first to invent paper, so it makes sense that they were the first to invent papier mâché. The modern name comes from French and means "chewed paper." Supposedly, French workers in English paper shops would chew on paper to moisten it so they could make papier mâché constructions. Papier mâché has been around such a long time, and it's a great material for constructing things because it's easy to work with, is lightweight, and can be painted. All you need to tackle a project is an idea, some newspaper, and some flour and water for the paste. Once you have these, whatever shape you can dream up can be created. Papier mâché masks can also make a great addition to a play, if you need more than just stage makeup for any of your characters.

SKILL LEVEL	◉ ◉
TIME NEEDED	2 days

THE PASTE

1 This is the basis of your papier mâché. You'll need to make plenty of it for any project you start.

2 Mix one part flour to about two parts water in a large mixing bowl. You're going for the consistency of gravy—not too thick and not too watery. If it's too thick,

it's difficult to work with. If it's too watery, it'll take your project forever to dry.

3 Stir the mixture until you get all the lumps out.

4 Add a tablespoon of salt for each part flour to prevent mold from growing on your models.

PAPIER MÂCHÉ MASK

1 This is a project anyone can do, though it takes some detailed work and about two days to complete, mostly because you have to let the

papier mâché dry. Papier mâché masks can be painted in any design you like, so they're great for spooky Halloween costumes.

YOU WILL NEED

A large mixing bowl

All-purpose flour

Salt

Water

A round balloon

Newspaper strips, roughly 2 in (5 cm) wide

An old bowl

Tinfoil

Masking tape

Paint

2 This is messy work so cover your work area with a plastic table cloth or sheets of newspaper.

3 Blow up the balloon to the desired size— you want it to be a bit larger than your head, so that you'll be able to fit the mask comfortably over your face when it's done.

4 Except for a head-sized hole in the bottom, cover the balloon with a layer of newspaper strips dipped in the paste. Hold one end of a newspaper strip and run it lengthways through the paste. As it comes out, use the thumb and forefinger of your other hand to squeeze off the excess paste.

5 Cover the whole thing in three layers of newspaper strips—any more than that and it'll take forever to dry. Then place the covered balloon in an old bowl, propped so that it stays upright, and leave it overnight to dry completely.

6 When the "head" has dried, repeat step 4 again with another three layers of papier mâché, and leave it to dry again.

7 When it has completely dried, pop the balloon. Now you should have a sturdy base for your mask. Put it over your head and carefully mark the positions of your eyes, nose, and mouth on the outside with a pencil. Take the mask off and poke the pencil through to make eye-, nose-, and mouth-holes.

8 Now use more papier mâché to model monstrous features around the eyes, nose, and mouth. Use your imagination to create something really scary! When it's dry, paint over the top to make a realistic monster face. The mask should now be ready to wear.

RUBBING LEAVES

While away a sunny afternoon with some fabulous leaf rubbing designs. With a little patience and a lot of imagination, you can produce some wonderful nature-themed patterns.

SKILL LEVEL	●
TIME NEEDED	20 minutes

YOU WILL NEED

2 sheets of plain white paper

A selection of leaves

A packet of colored crayons

1 Collect a selection of leaves in different shapes and sizes. Place the leaves, vein side up, on a sheet of white paper in any pattern you like, and put the second sheet of white paper on top of your design.

2 Take off any paper wrapping around your crayons. Using the long side of a crayon rather than the tip, rub gently over the sheet. The outline of your leaves will appear and reveal your designs.

3 We tend instinctively to turn to autumnal shades of browns, russets, and greens when leaf rubbing but you can actually use any color, however vibrant, in your design. Go crazy and see what works for you!

PERFORMING A PLAY

If you've had stars in your eyes since the very first time you appeared as an angel in the school nativity play, then join us as we slap on the greasepaint and head for center stage. With a few good friends, a little rehearsal, and a lot of fun, stage fright will be a thing of the past.

SKILL LEVEL ◉ ◉

TIME NEEDED   at least a few days

1 First choose the play. Are you drawn to the Classics, or a Shakespearean tragedy? Or do you prefer a modern drama such as an Arthur Miller play? Perhaps a comedy is more your thing. Or you could write your own play.

2 You'll have to gather your friends together and hold an audition to see who will play which part. You can get everyone to have a blind vote on who is best in the role.

3 It's time to start rehearsing the play. First, you should all sit around comfortably in a room and just read the script through in character. After a few read-throughs, you need to get on stage (or in your performance room) and start rehearsing with actions and real feeling. This gives you a great opportunity to refine techniques such as voice projection (how loud or soft you speak), use of props, positions, movements, and gestures,

remembering your lines, exits, and entrances, and general acting style.

4 Scenery and props can be a problem for amateur dramatic groups. Do you know a friend or even a kind parent who has creative flair? They may agree to paint some backdrops to make your play more convincing. If not, try to keep the performance area as uncluttered and neutral as possible.

5 A dress rehearsal, which is when you go through the play without an audience but in full costume, is your final chance to make sure everything fits and that your play is perfect.

6 And now, the big moment is here. The audience is seated, the curtain rises and the lights dim. Just try not to forget your lines!

YOU WILL NEED

A play of your choice

Enough friends to play all the parts

Scenery/props

Costumes

A stage area

FACE PAINTING

If you're performing in a play, or just want to add some spice to a Halloween costume or ghost story, knowing how to apply stage makeup is a great skill to have.

SKILL LEVEL	●
TIME NEEDED	20 minutes –½ hour

Stage makeup is normally thick and dramatic, and all actors—men and women! Wear it so that the audience can see their expressions even at the very back of the theater. The makeup also helps to stop the actors' faces from looking pale under the bright stage lighting. For amateur purposes, in a small room and without stage lighting, standard day makeup will be fine for your performance.

You can also use makeup for special effects, or to enhance someone's character on stage. To make someone look older, for example, lightly draw wrinkles at the corners of their eyes and mouth, and use a dusting of talcum powder to make their hair look gray. To make someone look thin and gaunt, add dark shadows under their eyes and in the hollows under their cheekbones. And for those dramatic moments, you can easily get hold of fake blood from a novelty store—just make sure it doesn't get anywhere it might stain!

YOU WILL NEED

Face paints or stage makeup in green, black, sparkly silver or gold, and sparkly white

A makeup sponge

A makeup brush

WITCH MAKEUP

1 Sometimes subtle and understated just doesn't do the trick, and nothing but old-fashioned, exaggerated face-painting will do. This witch look will be great for spooky performances at Halloween parties, the witches' roles in Macbeth, or any time you need to dress up.

2 Using a sponge, apply a fine layer of sparkly white face paint all over your face as a base for your design.

3 Again with a sponge, apply a covering of bright green around your forehead, the sides of your face, and your chin and nose. Blend it in with the base layer for a greenish-white tinge, rather than a complete covering.

4 Using a medium brush and black face paint, paint on some flamboyant wavy eyebrows. Fill in your lips with black and draw a thick line under your eyes, sweeping from the middle of each eye out toward the temples.

5 Add a spooky cobweb on one cheek in black paint, complete with spider.

6 Finally, outline some of the spider web with sparkly gold or silver face paint for a finishing touch.

DID YOU KNOW?

The Ancient Egyptians and Romans used makeup containing mercury and lead—both very toxic metals.

FEASTING

Food, glorious food! There's nothing quite as satisfying as rustling up your own delicious dishes for a summer feast. So this chapter is packed full of great ideas for fare that you can cook and eat outdoors such as BBQs, picnics, and campfire cooking, as well as some easy-to-follow recipes that will help even complete rookie cooks create great food for the summer season.

HOMEMADE LEMONADE

There's nothing more refreshing on a sweltering summer's day than homemade lemonade, and it's the perfect addition to any picnic. Once you've tasted this recipe, you'll never go back to store-bought lemonade again!

SKILL LEVEL ◉

TIME NEEDED 1 hour

YOU WILL NEED

1¼ cups (240 g) granulated sugar

6 cups (1.5 liters) cold water

A large saucepan

1 cup (250 ml) freshly squeezed lemon juice (about 5–8 lemons)

A pitcher (to serve)

1 Pour the sugar and 1 cup (250 ml) of the water into a saucepan. Gently bring to a boil on medium heat.

2 Once boiling, reduce to a simmer and stir until all the sugar has dissolved.

3 This syrup can now be put to one side to cool, then refrigerate for about half an hour.

4 Then mix the syrup with 5 cups (1.25 ml) of cold water. Add the fresh lemon juice. Mix well, serve with ice, and enjoy.

ZINGY ICED TEA

If you like hot tea but don't want it on a warm summer's day, reach for a cold, refreshing glass of iced tea.

SKILL LEVEL ◉

TIME NEEDED 10 minutes

YOU WILL NEED

5 cups (1.25 liters) of water

A medium-sized pan

5 green tea bags (you can use black tea bags but this gives a stronger flavor)

1 cup (200 g) sugar

A large pitcher

Iced water

Lemon slices (to garnish)

1 Bring 5 cups (1.25 liters) of water to a boil in a pan on the stove.

2 Drop in five tea bags and allow to boil for no more than a minute. Place to one side.

3 Add the sugar to a large pitcher. Pour in just enough hot water to melt the sugar.

4 Pour the hot tea from the pan into the pitcher, then remove the tea bags.

5 Fill the rest of the pitcher with ice-cold water. You can add lemon slices as a garnish if you like. Stir, serve, and enjoy!

SUMMER SMOOTHIES

If you find it hard to eat the recommended daily portions of fruit and vegetables, we've got the perfect solution—blitz all your favorite fruits together to make a smoothie packed full of goodness. Virtually any ripe fruit you find in the fruit bowl can be used—the combinations are endless and entirely up to you. And summer is such a time of plenty for fruit that you really can go crazy. It's a good idea to use bananas as a background to other fruits because they give your finished smoothie a good velvety texture. For a colorful smoothie, add any sort of berries, from blueberries to blackberries and mulberries.

SKILL LEVEL   ●

TIME NEEDED   10 minutes

1 Add the liquid ingredients to the blender.

2 Then add the rest of the ingredients, one at a time, blitzing briefly (sometimes called pulsing) in between each new addition to avoid clogging up the blender blade.

3 Check the consistency of your smoothie. If it's too thick, add more milk. Too thin, a little more yogurt.

4 Pour into a tall glass over ice cubes, add a straw, and maybe a strawberry for decoration if you like, and it's ready to drink.

YOU WILL NEED

A blender

A handful of strawberries

1 banana

⅔ cup (150 ml) vanilla yogurt

⅓ cup (75 ml) milk

⅓ cup (75 ml) orange juice

A handful of ice cubes

Strawberries for garnish

FRUITY ICE POPS

Kick off your shoes, sit on the porch, and chill out with these homemade ice pops. This recipe makes about 14 ice pops, so there are plenty for your family and friends if you feel like sharing.

SKILL LEVEL	◉
TIME NEEDED	4–5 hours

1 Place the blackcurrants, sugar, lemon zest, and juice in a pan with ⅓ cup (75 ml) water. Heat gently, stirring until the sugar dissolves, then bring to a boil. Simmer gently for 5 minutes, then allow to cool.

2 Purée the mixture with a hand-held electric whisk until smooth (or tip into a blender to liquidize). Stir in 1¼ cups (323 ml) chilled water.

3 Pour into molds and freeze for at least 4 hours, until solid.

4 No fresh fruit? You can use fresh fruit juice, diluted to about half and half, with water (or lemonade for a treat) in the molds.

YOU WILL NEED

1⅓ cup (200 g) blackcurrants

½ cup (100 g) superfine sugar

Grated zest and juice of one unwaxed lemon

A medium-sized pan

1½ cups (375 ml) water

Hand-held electric whisk or blender

Ice pop molds (available from stores)

DID YOU KNOW?

In 2005, a U.S. soft-drink maker, Snapple, attempted to beat the Dutch world record of a 21-foot (6.5-m) ice pop, as listed in the *Guinness Book of World Records*. Snapple tried to build a 25-foot (7.6-m) ice pop in New York, but the frozen juice melted faster than expected, and spectators fled to higher ground as fire fighters hosed away the mess!

TOP TIP

If you can't wait 4 hours, you can make mini ice pops by pouring your mixture into ice cube trays. Partially freeze, then place toothpicks in the center of each cube, and then freeze fully to make either mini ice pops, or colored and flavored ice cubes. If adding to drinks as ice cubes, remove toothpicks before serving.

PLANNING A PICNIC

Whether you're attending an outdoor concert, having a day at the beach or lake, or simply heading to your local park or out into your own backyard, eating *al fresco* (outdoors) is always a huge treat. So, forget the ants and wasps, pack a ball, a Frisbee, or a good book, and load up your picnic hamper with some of these fun-filled picnic ideas.

SKILL LEVEL	◉
TIME NEEDED	1–2 hours

Here are a few things to think about to make sure your day goes without a hitch:

SCALE: Is this picnic going to be a simple snack on the run or a fresh-air feast? Are you aiming for simplicity or to impress with gourmet dining?

GUESTS: Who is going to be at the picnic? If it's just you and your friends, why not suggest that each friend brings a favorite dish to share.

WEATHER: I know, I know...you can't change the weather, but you can take a few precautions. If it's hot, make sure your food is suitably chilled, and remember the sunscreen. If it's cloudy, a large umbrella can save the day.

NUTRITION: Picnic food should be fun but not entirely consisting of junk food, so make sure you pack some healthy food as well as treats. And don't forget something to drink!

COMFORT: No one wants to spend time sitting on wet grass or a hard rock. Pack a picnic rug or some lightweight camping chairs and you won't regret it.

FINGER FOODS: Try to choose foods that you can eat without cutlery—such as wraps—which will save on the amount you have to carry with you, and on the dish washing when you get home.

ENTERTAINMENT: Depending on your location, why not pack a ball, fishing rod, or Frisbee? Or take some cord to rig up a makeshift volleyball net or limbo.

BE CREATIVE: Why not be adventurous and take a barbecue or plan a campfire picnic? How about a theme picnic where both the outfits and food have to fit the theme?

FOOD IDEAS

Well that's enough to get you thinking about what sort of picnic you'd like to plan. Now, let's get down to basics and start thinking about the sort of food you'd like to enjoy on the day.

MAIN SNACKS: A picnic doesn't just have to be about sandwiches. If you want to make your picnic a little more interesting, and avoid the problem of soggy bread, you could substitute the simple sandwich with any of the following snacks:

Pasta, potato, or rice salad in a sealed container
Tortilla wraps with a favorite filling
Wholewheat crackers
Pizza slices
Mini pitas
Bagels
Sausage rolls
Dips

VEGETABLES: You can get your vegetable quota by adding salad items to a sandwich or wrap, or pack them separately in little pots. Try:

Cherry tomatoes
Cucumber chunks
Carrot and celery sticks
Sticks of red or green bell pepper

FRUIT: Fruit doesn't have to be boring. Why not include:

Grapes, strawberries, cherries, or any favorite fruit in a pot
Kiwi fruit (don't forget to take a spoon!)
Dried apricots, mixed fruits, raisins, or pineapple
Ring-pull cans of fruit in juice

TREATS: Every picnic needs a sweet treat. Any of the treats in this chapter, such as your own homemade iced cookies (see page 120) would be great but any cakes or pastries are fine.

FRUIT PICKING

What better way to spend family time on a summer's day than to spend a day picking fresh fruits that are bursting with flavor at this time of year? Grab a sunhat and a large basket, and head off to a Pick Your Own farm to find your favorite fruit. Just try not to eat too many as you pick or you'll end up going home empty-handed. Here are a few suggestions to make sure that your fruit picking goes without a hitch:

SKILL LEVEL	●
TIME NEEDED	20 minutes

SEASONAL FRUIT: Check out which fruits are in season before heading off. In early summer (July/August) you can find strawberries, raspberries, gooseberries, blueberries, cherries, rhubarb, redcurrants, and blackcurrants in abundance. Later in summer (August/September), look for apples, pears, plums, nectarines, raspberries, tayberries, and loganberries.

PICKING: If the fruits are low down, such as strawberries, vary your position to save yourself from getting a backache. Take care when picking fruits from prickly bushes, such as raspberries and gooseberries. A pair of thin gloves can save you from scratches.

HEALTH: It's only natural to pop the odd strawberry into your mouth while picking—after all, they are tantalizingly tasty—but try to keep your sampling to a minimum or you will inevitably end up with a stomachache if you eat too many.

SELECTING FRUIT: Only select the plump, fully ripened fruits. Unripe berries will not ripen once picked, so if they are still green or white in places, leave them on the plants.

QUANTITY: It's easy to get carried away when fruit picking (because it's such fun) and to end up with more produce than you can eat. If you do overpick, remember that fruits such as strawberries quickly go moldy when left at room temperature, and only last a couple of days in the refrigerator.

STORAGE: Most fresh berries such as strawberries, blueberries, and raspberries can be frozen. Take out what you need and the remainder can be washed; cut the hulls (stems) off strawberries, and then pop them into a ziplock bag, removing as much air as possible. The berries will keep for months frozen without air.

PREPARATION: Fresh picked fruit is delicious just as it is. If you have plenty, why not make a fresh fruit salad, or try your hand at making some homemade jam.

FRESH FRUIT SALAD

1 In a large bowl, whisk together the lime juice, honey, and mint.

2 Add all of the fruit and toss to combine.

3 Allow the flavors to blend for about 15 minutes before serving.

SKILL LEVEL	●
TIME NEEDED	20 minutes

YOU WILL NEED

A mixing bowl

4 tbsp fresh lime juice

4 tbsp liquid honey

A few sprigs of mint

A mixture of fresh berries such as blueberries, strawberries, and raspberries

3 apples, peeled, cored, and cut into chunks

STICKY STRAWBERRY JAM

1 Prepare the strawberries by removing all tops and greenery, and chop large fruits into chunks.

2 Put the strawberries and the lemon juice into the saucepan and simmer very gently for an hour.

3 Add the sugar and turn up the heat until the temperature rises to setting point (220°F/105°C).

4 Once the jam has reached setting point, skim any scum off the top of the jam. Set aside until a skin starts to form.

5 Pour into sterilized jars, seal them, and let cool. Label them and store in a cool place.

SKILL LEVEL	● ●
TIME NEEDED	2 hours

YOU WILL NEED

12 cups (1.5 kg) strawberries

Juice of one lemon

A large, heavy saucepan

5½ cups (1.25 kg) sugar

Sterilized jars

BAKING A PIE

Baking a pie may sound like something your mom used to do when she was a girl, but when you taste a slice of this heavenly peach pie, you'll realize that sometimes a bit of retro action in the kitchen may be just what's needed. Your family will certainly thank you for it.

SKILL LEVEL   ● ●

TIME NEEDED   40 minutes–1 hour

PEACH PIE

1 Roll out the pastry and fit it over your pie plate, trimming off any excess.

2 Prick the pastry all over before baking it in an oven at 375°F (190°C) until golden (about 20 minutes).

3 Meanwhile, blanch the peaches by putting them in a pan of boiling water for about 20 seconds, then emptying them out and pouring cold water over them. This loosens the skin so that they are easy to peel.

4 Cut the peaches into slices and discard the stones.

5 Place all but one of the sliced peaches in a saucepan together with a cup of water. Keep one peach in reserve for later.

YOU WILL NEED

Ready-to-roll short pastry

4–5 large freestonepeaches

Water

½ cup (100 g) of sugar

A saucepan

Cornstarch

A ceramic, glass, or metal pie pan

A rolling pin

A fork

Oven mitts

DID YOU KNOW?

Partially cooking pastry for a pie or flan without any filling is known as "blind" baking.

6 Place on medium heat, mashing occasionally with a potato masher or fork. Add the sugar, turn down heat, and simmer for about 10 minutes.

7 In a cup, mix 3 tablespoons of cornstarch with ⅔ cup (166 ml) of cold water.

8 Bring the fruit mixture back to a boil and slowly stir in the cornstarch-and-water mixture.

9 Cook until the mixture is clear and thickened.

10 Take off the heat and allow the mixture to cool slightly.

11 Decorate the base of the pie crust with the last peach, which you've peeled and sliced but not cooked.

12 Pour the cooled fruit mixture over the top and refrigerate. The pie-to-die-for is ready to serve whenever you and your guests (you mean you're going to share?!) want to eat.

FUDGE

Fudge is the perfect little sweet treat; great for an energy boost or as a gift for your friends.

SKILL LEVEL	◉ ◉
TIME NEEDED	½ hour–30 minutes

YOU WILL NEED

3 cups (750 g) chocolate chips

1 cup (250 ml) condensed milk

1 teaspoon of vanilla extract

A microwave or stone

A microwave-safe bowl or measuring cup

A square baking pan between 7 and 9 in (17 and 23 cm) across

Aluminum/tin foil to line the tin

A metal spoon

A spatula

1 Line the pan with the aluminum foil. Pour the chocolate chips into the bowl or measuring cup and add the condensed milk and vanilla extract.

2 Put the bowl in the microwave and heat for 1–3 minutes. Stir the mixture and pour it into the foil-lined pan, using the spatula to level it.

3 Put the fudge in the refrigerator. After 15–20 minutes, it should be ready for cutting into squares about 1 inch (2.5 cm) in size.

4 Let it cool further, then put in a sealed plastic container and store in the fridge.

LEMON TART

The zing of lemon makes this simple but delicious tart less rich than some desserts but it's sugary enough to satisfy the most demanding sweet tooth. Better still, it looks very sophisticated when served, so it's an all round winner.

SKILL LEVEL ⬤ ⬤

TIME NEEDED 5 hours

1 Preheat the oven to 425°F (220°C).

2 Roll the pastry thinly. Cut into big enough circle to fit flan pan. Loosely wrap pastry over rolling pin to transport over tin. Press gently into pan and cut off surplus.

3 Prick the base of tart and line with baking parchment and a few baking beans. Bake till golden (8–10 minutes). Remove the paper and beans. Cool.

4 Mix the lemon curd and crème fraîche and then pour into the flan tin.

5 Dip the redcurrants in the egg white, then into the sugar. Leave to dry, then place in the middle of the tart.

6 For an extra touch of class, add curls of lemon zest as a garnish, and serve.

YOU WILL NEED

FOR THE TART:

9 oz (250 g) ready-made short pastry

Rolling pin

Flan pan

Parchment paper and dried beans

4 tbsp lemon curd

2 tbsp crème fraîche or sour cream

TO DECORATE:

Small bunch redcurrants

1 egg white, lightly beaten

Caster sugar to frost

Curls of lemon zest to garnish

NO-BAKE CHEESECAKE

Cheesecake is one of the best-loved desserts all over the world. This delicious citrus cheesecake can be made with the minimum of fuss and with no need to use an oven.

SKILL LEVEL	◉ ◉
TIME NEEDED	5 hours

1 Crush the graham crackers roughly by sealing them in a plastic food bag and bashing them with a wooden spoon or rolling pin.

2 Place the crushed crackers in the bowl and mix in the melted butter.

3 Put the mixture into the pan and, using the back of the spoon, spread it evenly and then press it down to form the base.

4 Put the pan into the fridge to set (about 30 minutes).

5 In a bowl, mix cream cheese, orange zest, ricotta, sugar, and milk.

6 Put the cream in a clean bowl and whisk until it is thick. Add to the orange mixture and blend thoroughly.

7 Remove pan from the fridge. Pour the filling over the cracker base and spread evenly.

8 Decorate with segments of orange, if desired, and return to the fridge for at least 4 hours before serving.

YOU WILL NEED

15 graham crackers

A rolling pin or wooden spoon

6 tbsp (85 g) butter, melted

1⅔ cups (400 g) cream cheese

Grated zest of 3 oranges (use the segments for decoration)

¾ cup (200 g) ricotta cheese

½ cup (100 g) superfine sugar

3 tbsp milk

¾ cup (184 ml) heavy cream

9-in (23-cm) nonstick springform pan

Mixing bowl

DID YOU KNOW?

Historians believe that cheesecake was served to the athletes during the first Olympic Games held in 776 B.C. At that time, cheesecake would have been made using curd cheese because cream cheese wasn't invented until 1872, when it was accidentally discovered by American dairyman William Lawrence of Chester, N.Y., while trying to emulate a soft French cheese called Neufchatel.

TOP TIP

This cheesecake is much easier to make if you leave the cream cheese out of the fridge to soften for a couple of hours before mixing.

ANGEL CUPCAKES

These are the prettiest cupcakes you can make, not to mention the most delicious. For a special occasion, such as a birthday party, why not arrange them on a three-tier display where they will look irresistible?

SKILL LEVEL	● ●
TIME NEEDED	1 hour

1 Preheat the oven to 325°F (170°C).

2 Put all cake ingredients in a bowl and mix using a hand-mixer (or a wooden spoon if you're feeling strong).

3 Line a 12-hole muffin pan with paper baking cups. Divide the batter into each cup, making them about two-thirds full.

4 Using oven mitts, carefully place the muffin pan in the pre-heated oven on the middle shelf for about 30 minutes.

YOU WILL NEED

FOR THE CAKES:

2 medium eggs

1 cup (110 g) self-rising flour

1–2 tsp baking powder

7 tbsp (110 g) soft butter

½ cup (110 g) sugar

A large mixing bowl

An electric hand-mixer or wooden spoon

12 paper baking cups

A 12-hole muffin pan

A pair of oven mitts

FOR BUTTER ICING:

1⅓ cup (170 g) powdered sugar

6 tbsp (85 g) soft butter

3 drops vanilla extract

1 tbsp milk

WARNING

Take great care when handling sharp knives and use oven mitts when handling hot muffin pans.

5 Transfer pan to a wire cooling rack. When cool, remove the baking cups. Using a sharp knife, slice off the top part of each one, then cut the sliced section in two—these will be used later to form your angel wings.

6 Place all the ingredients for the butter icing in a large bowl and stir for about 5 minutes until well combined.

7 Place a teaspoon of butter icing on top of each cupcake. Then push the "wings" into the butter icing.

8 Dust with powdered sugar for an "angelic" final touch.

TOP TIP

When your cupcakes are in the oven, do not open the oven door to check on them for at least 20 minutes or your cupcakes may collapse. They are cooked when golden brown.

HOMEMADE ICE CREAM

This recipe is for vanilla ice cream, but there are plenty of other flavorings you can use, such as strawberry or mint.

SKILL LEVEL	◉ ◉
TIME NEEDED	4 hours

YOU WILL NEED

2 mixing bowls

A whisk

4 eggs (separated)

½ cup (110 g) sugar

1 ¼ cups (300 ml) whipping cream

Vanilla extract

Large plastic container

1 Whisk the egg yolks in a bowl until they are blended.

2 Whisk egg whites in a separate, larger bowl until they form soft peaks.

3 Whisk in the sugar, a teaspoon at a time. The whites will get stiffer as the sugar is added.

4 Blend in the egg yolks until no streaks or color remain.

5 Whisk the cream until it forms soft peaks and then fold into mixture.

6 Add a few drops of vanilla extract. Pour mixture into a container, cover, and freeze.

ICED COOKIES

These cookies are so quick and easy to make that you can spend longer having fun with the icing bag and adding decorations. Be adventurous with your decorations— intricate patterns, bright colors, you can even pop a fresh strawberry on top to add a seasonal flourish. This recipe will make about 20 cookies.

SKILL LEVEL ◉ ◉

TIME NEEDED   1 hour

1 Preheat oven to 375°F (190°C).

2 Place the butter and sugar into a mixing bowl and beat.

3 Add beaten egg gradually, beating all the time.

4 Add flour and vanilla extract and mix it again until you can make it into a ball of dough.

5 Lightly flour a work surface and roll out dough until it's about ½ inch (1.25 cm) thick.

YOU WILL NEED

FOR THE COOKIES:

7 tbsp (100 g) soft unsalted butter

½ cup (110 g) superfine sugar

1 egg, beaten

2½ cups (275 g) all-purpose flour

2 drops vanilla extract

A hand-mixer or food processor

Cookie cutters

A nonstick cookie sheet

Oven mitts

A wire rack

TO DECORATE:

3 cups (400 g) powdered sugar

A large bowl

Various food colorings

Small candies, fresh fruit, edible silver balls

A palette knife or spatula

6 Use cookie cutters to make attractive shapes out of the dough, then place cookies onto a nonstick cookie sheet.

7 Bake in preheated oven for about 10 minutes until lightly golden on the edges.

8 Wearing oven mitts, remove from oven carefully, and leave to harden for 2 minutes. Then lift each cookie onto a wire rack using a spatula and allow to cool.

9 Make icing by sifting powdered sugar into a large bowl.

10 Gradually add enough warm water to make a soft, firm mixture (usually about 2–3 tablespoons). This is the icing.

11 Divide icing according to how many food colorings you have. Add a half teaspoon of coloring to each icing batch and mix well.

12 Spread the icing onto cookies using a metal spatula. Then decorate to your heart's content.

FRUIT GELATIN

Anyone can make a gelatin using a package, but it's much more satisfying to make a gelatin from scratch. And you can vary this recipe according to what fruits are in season.

SKILL LEVEL	◉ ◉
TIME NEEDED	2–3 hours

YOU WILL NEED

2 cups (500 ml) red grape juice

A small saucepan

4 tsp powdered gelatin

A handful of red grapes

Individual serving bowls

1 Put 6 tablespoons of grape juice into a small saucepan and slowly sprinkle the gelatin powder over it. Set aside for between 5–10 minutes.

2 Return the saucepan to a low heat and allow the gelatin to melt slowly—do not let it boil.

3 Gradually stir in the remaining grape juice, making sure it is well blended.

4 Wash, halve, and deseed grapes. Arrange them in the bottom of individual party bowls.

5 Pour the gelatin mixture over the grapes. Place in the fridge until just starting to set. Top with more grape halves, then return to fridge to set fully.

BRILLIANT BBQS

Think of summer food and the first thing that springs to mind is a barbecue—the perfect meal for lighter evenings and parties outside. Whether you spend hours preparing marinades or spontaneously throw a few hotdogs on the grill, a barbecue is the ideal way to cook up a feast.

SKILL LEVEL	◉
TIME NEEDED	10 minutes

BARBECUE SAUCE

Favorite dishes for barbecue-lovers include hotdogs, hamburgers, chicken, kebabs, steaks, and fish. If you want to help with the preparation, most meat can be spiced up with this easy-to-make marinade:

1 Put the ketchup into a bowl with the lemon juice.

2 Add the vinegar, mix thoroughly.

3 Then stir in all of the remaining ingredients.

4 Spread the sauce onto the food before it goes onto the barbecue. Really, it's that simple!

YOU WILL NEED

A medium mixing bowl

¾ cup (200 ml) tomato ketchup

Juice of one lemon

⅔ cup (150 ml) red wine vinegar

6 cloves garlic, minced

4 tbsp maple syrup

2 tbsp olive oil

2 tbsp wholegrain mustard

4 tbsp chopped fresh parsley

WARNINGS

• It's very important to make sure that cooked meat is piping hot all the way through, including in the middle. Even if it's burnt black on the outside that doesn't mean it's cooked properly on the inside. If your meat is pink at all, get an adult to put it back on for a little longer.

• Don't run around near a hot barbecue and remember also that it takes a long time to cool down after use.

• Have a bucket of water handy at all times, just in case.

DELICIOUS DESSERT IDEAS

Thread 2 or 3 large marshmallows onto the end of a wooden skewer. Hold the skewer over glowing embers until the outside of the marshmallows is crisp. (Be careful: the inside can be very hot and sticky.)

Place whole bananas in their skins on the barbecue until blackened. Then scoop out the hot flesh with a spoon. For a special treat, slice the banana along its length and add chunks of chocolate before cooking.

Thread chunks of your favorite fruits onto a skewer for a hot fruit kebab.

CAMPFIRE COOKING

It's a bizarre fact that food cooked outdoors always tastes better. Perhaps it's because everyone is ravenous from all the fresh air. Whatever the reason, and whether you're having a campfire in your backyard, or you're actually going camping with friends or family, knowing how to cook a meal on a campfire is a really useful skill.

SKILL LEVEL	● ● ●
TIME NEEDED	1½ hour

COOKING OUTDOORS

When camping out, you use the fire to boil water, and then let the flames die down and use the embers and hot ash for cooking. The embers don't burn so fiercely, so they'll cook your meal evenly all the way through. Trying to cook on flames will turn your food into a blackened mess on the outside, and leave it raw in the middle! Always make sure your food is properly cooked before eating it. Some foods such as chicken or fish can be cooked directly in the embers of a fire, wrapped in foil to stop them from burning (see recipes on opposite page). Otherwise you can use sharpened sticks for a skewer (ideal for vegetable kebabs) or as a toasting fork (good for sausages, toast, and marshmallows). If you're lucky enough to have a pot or billycan, here's how to make a pot rest so you can cook a proper meal.

YOU WILL NEED

2 sturdy forked sticks

A longer, straight stick, also reasonably strong

A pot

An open fire

1 Drive the base of a sturdy, forked stick into the ground near the fire, and another one on the opposite side of the fire.

2 Rest a longer stick across the two forks so it rests over the fire. The trick is to get forked sticks that are long enough so that your crosspiece doesn't catch fire!

3 Hang your can from the crosspiece so it sits close to the heat of the embers. Now you're ready to start cooking.

4 Add whatever ingredients you like to your pot. For a one-pot delight, add chopped vegetables, some meat, a stock cube and some water and leave it to stew. If you can't face all the peeling and chopping, simply drop a boil-in-the-bag dinner into some boiling water. Bon appetit!

CHICKEN DINNER FOR TWO

1 Place a chicken breast on a sheet of foil. Top with half of your chosen vegetables. Then season with salt and pepper. Repeat with other chicken breast.

2 Wrap up in foil and use second sheet to cover securely. At same time, wrap up each cob of corn, dotted with butter, in foil.

3 Using tongs, place wrapped chicken and corn directly on the coals of a campfire and let cook for about 15–20 minutes.

4 Turn occasionally and check chicken is cooked through by testing with a knife—the juices should run clear—before serving.

YOU WILL NEED

A campfire

2 chicken breasts

Aluminum foil

3 cups (450 g) assorted cut-up vegetables (e.g., carrot slices, chopped onion, sliced mushrooms, sliced zucchini)

Salt and pepper

2 cobs of corn

Stick of butter

Barbecue tongs

BANANA DESSERT

1 Slit a banana down the middle while it is still in the peel.

2 Sprinkle brown sugar, broken pieces of chocolate bar or chocolate chips, and tiny marshmallows into the slit.

3 Wrap up in foil and warm for several minutes in coals.

4 Remove it from the coals using tongs and serve.

YOU WILL NEED

A campfire

A banana

Aluminum foil

1 tbsp brown sugar

Chocolate bar or package of chocolate chips

Packet of mini marshmallows

TOP TIP

Foods such as fish and chicken can be cooked directly in the embers of a fire, wrapped in aluminum foil. Or you can skewer vegetables on sticks for kebabs or cook sausages on sticks like a toasting fork.

WARNINGS

- Be careful on opening foil. The steam coming out will be very hot.
- Be careful around a campfire. Keep hands and feet away from fire.
- When cooking on a campfire, use long potholders or barbecue tongs and get an adult to help.
- After use, make sure your campfire is totally extinguished. Sprinkle water or dirt on the fire and embers and stir the ashes around with a stick.

SORBETS AND SLUSHIES

Perfect to serve at any party, sorbets and slushies make the ideal summer dessert or nonalcoholic cocktail (often called mocktails). Serve them with a sprig of mint or a sugar-frosted strawberry for an extra dash of flair and style.

SKILL LEVEL	◉ ◉
TIME NEEDED	4–5 hours

WATERMELON SORBET

1 Place water and sugar in a small saucepan. Bring the mixture to a boil, then lower the heat and simmer it gently for 5 minutes. Pour the liquid into the baking dish.

2 Blitz the watermelon chunks in a blender, then strain the resulting purée into a large bowl. Measure out 2 cups (500 ml) of the watermelon juice and stir it into the sugar syrup. Then add the lemon juice.

3 Place the tray in the freezer for 1 hour. Remove and

stir the mixture with a wooden spoon. Then refreeze for another 45 minutes.

4 Remove and stir once more, and then allow the mixture to freeze through (probably another couple hours).

5 Remove dish and allow ice to thaw slightly so that you can transfer it to a chilled blender. Pulse the machine just until the ice is slightly soft, occasionally scraping down the sides.

YOU WILL NEED

1 cup (250 ml) water

½ cup (100 g) sugar

A small saucepan

Pyrex baking dish, approx. 8 in (20 cm) square

4 cups (600 g) watermelon chunks

A blender

A sieve

A large mixing bowl

1½ tbsp lemon juice

COLA SLUSHIES

1 Pour 1 can of cola into a blender.

2 Add enough ice to cover and blitz.

3 Pour into glasses, add a straw, and presto! A delicious slushie.

YOU WILL NEED

1 can cola

A blender

Ice

SKILL LEVEL	◉
TIME NEEDED	10 minutes

OUTDOOR SUMMER PARTIES

Summer is undoubtedly the best time of year to make the most of being in the backyard. Why not get the whole family involved in organizing a themed party—just for you or invite your friends along too. Get everyone in the family to write out a plan for a themed backyard party (make sure it includes ideas for decoration, food, and entertainment). Put all of the ideas in a hat, and every time you're in the mood for a fun summer party, pick an idea out of the hat at random. If you do this every couple of weeks over the summer, everyone in the family will get a chance for his or her idea to be used. Here are some ideas to get you started:

SKILL LEVEL	◉
TIME NEEDED	1–2 hours

JUNGLE SAFARI

Make face masks out of cardboard in the shape of different animals (lions, elephants, giraffes, monkeys).

Make a picnic, jungle-style—use animal cookie cutters to make sandwiches in different animal shapes and make jungle cookies too.

Make up a pitcher of Jungle Juice by mixing orange, pineapple, and mango juice to make a tropical drink. You could also add chopped fruit and serve with ice and jungle-themed straws.

FAIRY FESTIVAL

Make a set of wings and a wand for all the family to wear to the fairy festival—and yes, dads and brothers have to join in!

Hang up tiny lights, play some tinkly fairy music, and use a bubble machine to fill the yard with bubbles.

Have a tea party using a doll's tea set. Serve sandwiches, carrot sticks, and angel cupcakes (see page 118).

How about some face painting to give everyone special mystical faces full of flowers and ivy?

COWBOYS AND INDIANS

Raid the costume cupboard for any cowboys and Indians outfits you might have. If you don't have anything, see if dad's got an old plaid shirt and a hat you can wear for a cowboy and an old t-shirt that you could fray at the bottom for an Indian. You could even make an Indian headdress with feathers stuck to a cardboard headband.

See if you can get hold of any bales of hay from a nearby farm to decorate the backyard and set up separate camps for the cowboys and Indians.

This theme is ideal for a barbecue feast (see page 122) so ask a parent to get the barbecue out and grill up some hotdogs, hamburgers, and corn on the cob.

Make a pitcher of homemade lemonade (see page 106)—a perfect accompaniment for barbecued food.

INDEX